HEAR IT AND SING IT
Singing in Tune!

WORKOUTS FOR THE CONTEMPORARY SINGER

JUDY NIEMACK

To access audio, visit:
www.halleonard.com/mylibrary

Enter Code
3008-6078-7742-1724

AUDIO TRACK LISTING

All track numbers are shown on the Contents page and also on each music page. Track numbers not in boxes are short examples. Tracks labeled with white track numbers in black boxes indicate my vocal examples, where I sing the example three times, then you should take over. Tracks shown with black numbers in white boxes are without my voice, and you can experiment and practice improvising on your own.

SECOND FLOOR MUSIC

EXCLUSIVELY DISTRIBUTED BY
HAL•LEONARD®
7777 W. BLUEMOUND RD. P.O. BOX 13819 MILWAUKEE, WI 53213

Vocals, text and exercises: Judy Niemack

Pianist: Andy Ezrin

Recorded by Michael Brorby at Acoustic Sound, Brooklyn, NY

Mastered by Jeanfrançois Prins

Music engraving by Osho Endo, book design by Maureen Sickler

Edited by Don Sickler and Elijah Shiffer

Cover: Christopher Drukker

ISBN 979-8350102949

Second Floor Music, 130 West 28th Street, floor 2, New York, N.Y. 10001 U.S.A. www.secondfloormusic.com

A Don Sickler Production

Exclusively Distributed By

HAL•LEONARD®

7777 W. Bluemound Rd. P.O. Box 13819 Milwaukee, WI 53213

HEAR IT AND SING IT
Singing in Tune!

Workouts for the Contemporary Singer

JUDY NIEMACK

page .... *audio track*

page		short example	black box	white box
5	**ABOUT THE BOOK**			
	SECTION 1: WARM UPS			
9	Conscious Breathing		1	
9	Hums		2	3
10	Hummin' ATriad		4	
12	Swingin' A Triad		5	
	SECTION 2: CHROMATIC WORKOUTS			
16	Chromatic Intervals		6	
18	Chromatic Intervals Using Solfege Syllables		7	
20	Chromatic Intervals with Interval Names		8	
22	Aeolian Ooh ah		9	
24	Minor Second	10	11	12
26	Major Second	13	14	15
28	Minor Third	16	17	18
30	Major Third	19	20	21
32	Perfect Fourth	22	23	24
34	Augmented Fourth	25	26	27
35	Perfect Fifth	28	29	30
36	Minor Sixth	31	32	33
38	Major Sixth	34	35	36
40	Minor Seventh	37	38	39
42	Major Seventh	40	41	42
44	Octave	43	44	45
	SECTION 3: ARPEGGIOS			
46	Major Seventh Arpeggios		46	
48	Major Ninth Arpeggios		47	
50	Major Sharp Eleventh Arpeggios		48	
51	Major Thirteenth Arpeggios		49	
52	Dominant Seventh Arpeggios		50	
54	Dominant Ninth Arpeggios		51	
56	Dominant Sharp Eleventh Arpeggios		52	
57	Dominant Thirteenth Arpeggios		53	
58	**EXAMPLES FROM THE REPERTOIRE**			
60	**ABOUT JUDY NIEMACK**			
62	**JUDY NIEMACK DISCOGRAPHY**			

Audio track numbers without boxes are short examples. Track numbers in black boxes indicate full length examples, where I sing the phrases three times, then you should take over.
Track numbers in white boxes are without my voice.

About the Book

"Singing in Tune" is a collection of vocal work outs designed specifically for the pop and jazz vocalist. In the course of almost fifty years of teaching vocal technique and jazz singing, I've developed many exercises to help singers get in shape and sing in tune. Here is some background on my vocal training and what led me to write this book, followed by some advice on how to use it.

As a child, singing was my joy. It later became my life. I started in a church choir at the age of seven, and sang in musicals, folk, blue-grass and madrigal groups, as well as in a rock band. All was well, until the morning after the big high school dance, where I'd been wailing Janis Joplin songs, and woke up with no voice! I soon found Primo Lino Puccinelli, who taught "Bel Canto" singing, and through him became fascinated with classical music. This led me to pursue conservatory training, where I focused on singing art songs and opera until I was twenty-two. To the dismay of the vocal department chairman, I was also singing jazz in clubs, and was sternly advised to choose one or the other or I'd "lose my voice". I wanted to explore the creative opportunities offered in jazz music and decided to make that my focus. Through the years, I've modified my classical technique to be able sing jazz, pop, broadway and in fact, whatever style I choose! I'm glad to say that I still have the same accuracy, range and flexibility that I had as a young singer (with the addition of a couple of low notes), and that thirty-five years after being a student there, I was invited back to New England Conservatory to teach a vocal jazz masterclass. My joy in singing and teaching is as strong as ever, and I am excited to share this method with you—because it works!

The basic building block of Western music is the half step (or "semitone"). If you can sing half steps in tune, throughout your entire range, with a variety of lyrics and melodies, you are well on your way to perfect intonation on songs. The next steps are scales, intervals and arpeggios, all of which are included in the exercises here. Of course, there is no substitute for having lessons with a good voice teacher; live interaction and feedback is invaluable. However, we singers have many so technical areas to master—intonation, range, flexibility and diction— that I felt it was time to create a way for jazz and pop singers to train these skills on their own. With "Hear it and Sing it! Singing in Tune" these essential abilities can be trained simultaneously in a new set of workouts that make practicing fun.

I've found that the most efficient and enjoyable way for vocal students to practice is by using call-and-response, which I call "Hear it and Sing it!" (See page 63 for more information on my other "Hear it and Sing it!" books). I've recorded lots of examples and accompaniment tracks for "Hear it and Sing it! Singing In Tune", and with the code found in the book you can start right in listening and repeating what you've heard, singing along with the piano accompaniment.

The exercises are in comfortable keys for most women's voices, but you can also change the keys and tempos on each track to fit your individual needs. It's not necessary to play the piano or even to read the music provided in the book, but if you are interested in improving your sight-singing skills, I'd recommend following the music while you practice. You'll find tips about what to focus on for each exercise. Each is progressively more challenging, with varied chord progressions and rhythmic grooves to keep things interesting. The goal is to enjoy the process as you master each step!

Section 1. is a daily warm up, beginning with conscious breathing and moving on to exercises and vocalises based on intervals and arpeggios. You'll focus on vowels and syllables rather than on the lyrics, allowing you to work on technical issues like posture, support, vowels and resonance as you focus on developing a consistent timbre throughout your range. After singing these, you'll be warmed up and ready for the chromatic workouts that follow.

Section 2. consists of twelve chromatic workouts based on each of the twelve intervals in an octave. These workouts gradually increase in complexity, starting with a semitone and adding a half step at a time, training intonation and pronunciation simultaneously. The lyrics were chosen carefully, and combine specific consonants and vowels that will help you to bridge register shifts (or "breaks") in your voice. With English words that are often mispronounced by non-native speakers, you'll find phrases about life and music, as well as some designed to provoke a smile. Each one has a specific technical purpose. There are written explanations above each of the exercises but the most important thing is to simply listen and repeat what you hear. Include these exercises in your daily practice to improve your pitch and diction.

Section 3. includes eight exercises designed to increase your range while training your ear. You'll be singing arpeggiated major and dominant seventh chords (the root, third, fifth and seventh degrees of the major and dominant scales) throughout your range, progressively adding the ninths, elevenths and thirteenths ("color notes" or "extensions"). As you sing along, you'll train your high notes, expand your range and become more comfortable with the harmonic colors commonly used in jazz.

In the appendix at the end of the book, you'll find a list of songs rom various genres, all with beautiful melodies. Each one contains a chromatic passage that can be used as practice material when sung in various keys throughout your range. Look for recordings of them to become familiar with the sound of the chromatic scales in songs.

I've developed these workouts over several years with students in Germany, Spain, Denmark, Finland, The Netherlands and the United States. Many thanks to all my cheerful "guinea pigs"!

Sincere thanks to Maureen Sickler at Second Floor Music for her work in realizing this project, to Don Sickler for producing it and to recording engineers Michael Brorby and Jeanfrançois Prins.

I hope you find many hours of enjoyment with this new practice method!

Judy Niemack

PREPARE TO SING

Why do we warm up? Gentle warm ups loosen muscles, shake excess mucous off the vocal folds and increase circulation to the larynx, reducing the risk of injury. It's important to stretch and then relax the muscles used in singing, just like we do before running or working out.

Start with some basic stretches to get your blood flowing:

1. Inhale slowly through your nose as you raise your hands over your head, palms facing upwards, clasping your hands at the top, and stretch, turning the palms towards the ceiling. Release the hands, palms facing down, and exhale slowly through the mouth with the sound of "sh" as you lower your arms to your sides. Imagine the shoulder blades moving towards each other as your arms descend. Repeat several times.

2. Slowly curl forwards, bending down until your head and arms are relaxed and hanging towards the floor. Imagine your hips reaching up to the ceiling as your head hangs downwards. Shake your head gently "Yes" and "No" to be sure you are not holding tension in the neck, and relax, breathing in through the nose and out through the mouth several times.

3. Bend your knees and rise up slowly with your head hanging down until the last moment. Feel each of your vertebrae uncurl, one by one, until you are standing upright

4. Slowly pull your shoulders up to your ears as you breathe in, then roll them forwards as you exhale. Repeat, rolling them backwards. Repeat.

5. Climb an imaginary rope ladder with huge steps, taking steps with your feet and grabbing the imaginary rope with your hands as you look up to the sky.

6. Stretch out your left arm as you gently pull your fingertips backwards and upwards. Let your head fall to your right shoulder. Extend the stretch of the neck muscles by gently pulling your head downwards with the right arm. Repeat on the other side, stretching out the right atm, and dropping the head to your left. Breathe in, then slowly roll your head down towards your chest as you exhale. Extend the stretch with a gentle pull downwards with your hands on the back of your head, elbows forward. Release and slowly return to standing position, elbows back, as you inhale. Repeat several times.

Section 1: VOCAL WARM UPS

1 **Conscious breathing.** Calm your body and mind as you focus your attention on the breath before beginning your actual singing practice. If you're standing, take a "noble" posture by stretching your arms overhead, then circling them back and down, keeping the chest slightly raised. If standing is difficult, sit up straight on a firm chair with your legs uncrossed and feet flat on the floor. Notice the movement of the chest, ribs and abdominal area as you breathe through the nose.

Practice slowly raising your arms out to the sides, palms up, and overhead as you inhale, and lowering them, palms down, as you exhale. The shoulders remain back and down, the head remains level and the shoulder blades should move towards each other.

2 **Hums.** Start with four slow conscious breaths, in through the nose and out through the mouth, then hum along with my voice or improvise your own melody along with it.

3 **Sing along track.** Here's a space to use whatever sounds or words feel right to you, creating a new warm up every day. Try using lip buzzes ("brrr"), tongue trills ("rrrr"), or the "ng" sound for a gentle warm up, or make up your own words. How do you feel today? Check in on your physical and emotional state and let your sound center you for the day.

This exercise is sung on the fifth, third and tonic of a Major scale: a Major triad. Close the lips loosely and feel the vibration in them as you hum along. As in all the exercises, I'll sing the exercise three times and then you'll be free to continue on your own!

4

Hummin' A Triad

JUDY NIEMACK

Amaj7
E7sus
Amaj7
B♭m7
E♭7
Mmm_
A♭maj7
E♭7sus
A♭maj7
Am7
D7
Mmm_
Gmaj7
D7sus
Gmaj7
A♭m7
D♭7
Mmm_
G♭maj7
D♭7sus
G♭maj7
Gm7
C7
Mmm_
Fmaj7
C7sus
Fmaj7

Here's a variation of the previous exercise, with a chromatic approach note added between each chord tone. If you want to really feel the swing groove, walk or step in place on the first and third beats and snap your fingers on the second and fourth beats while you sing. The first note of each phrase falls on the "up-beat." Give it a bit of energy!

5

Swingin' A Triad

(Dmaj7) A13sus Dmaj7 E♭m7 A♭ D♭maj7
doo doo doo doo doo doo doo Doo
(D♭maj7) A♭13sus D♭maj7 Dm7 G Cmaj7
doo doo doo doo doo doo doo Doo
(Cmaj7) G13sus Cmaj7 C♯m7 F♯ Bmaj7
doo doo doo doo doo doo doo Doo
(Bmaj7) F♯13sus Bmaj7 Cm7 F B♭maj7
doo doo doo doo doo doo doo Doo
(B♭maj7) F13sus B♭maj7
doo doo doo doo doo doo
Piano

Section 2 CHROMATIC WORKOUTS

What is a Chromatic scale?

"Chromatic" stems from the Greek word khromatikos, from khroma, or color.* Chromaticism adds color to diatonic melodies and creates tension and release. Using chromatic intervals in songwriting or improvising adds color or tension to diatonic melodies, which are generally "easy listening."

A chromatic scale consists of an ascending or descending sequence of twelve pitches progressing by semitones. You can produce this scale by sequentially playing each black and white key on a piano. The structure of a chromatic scale is therefore symmetrical throughout, unlike scales which have tones and semitones in particular arrangements, like major and minor scales.

What is a semitone?

The half step or semitone is the smallest interval and the most important building block of Western tonal music. It is defined as the interval between two adjacent notes in a 12-tone scale (e.g. from C to C♯). One octave consist of twelve semitones.

Where can I hear the Chromatic Scale?

Chromatic scales and runs can be found in many beautiful songs in the traditional vocal jazz repertoire. "Midnight Sun" (Hampton, Burke, Mercer), "Blue Monk" (Monk), "Sophisticated Lady" (Ellington, Parish), and Woody Herman's theme song "Early Autumn" (Burns, Mercer) are some good examples. Although contemporary pop tunes seldom make use of chromatic scales, there are a few famous pop songs where they are found, including "The Alley Cat Song" (Bjorn, Harlen), and Stevie Wonder's "Don't You Worry 'Bout a Thing." Brazilian pop music is full of chromaticism, for example in Antonio Carlos Jobim's "Zingaro" or "How Insensitive" (which is actually based on a classical piece—Frédéric Chopin's "Prelude in E-Minor, op. 28 no. 4").

* Collins English Dictionary - Complete & Unabridged 2012 Digital Edition © William Collins Sons & Co. Ltd. 1979, 1986 © HarperCollins

The study of chromatic scales has long been a part of classical instruction, to improve flexibility and intonation on both instruments and voices, as well as to prepare for some of the more challenging literature in classical music. In the century since its composition, Rimsky Korsakov's "Flight of the Bumblebee" has become a standard showcase for solo instrumental virtuosity, whether on the violin or on practically any other melodic instrument. Even "The Swingle Singers" recorded it! If you've heard the Habañera from George Bizet's "Carmen" or Pietro Mascagni's Intermezzo from "Cavalleria Rusticana" you've heard the chromatic scale. Although there are several books available for classical singers that feature chromatic studies, there has been nothing, up to now, written specifically for the Pop or Jazz vocalist. I developed these exercises to focus on accurately hearing and singing these basic building bocks of Western music.

Why study chromatic intervals and scales?

Being able to sing and hear every interval in an octave is essential for precise intonation. When your half steps are in tune, larger intervals will become secure. Simply by practicing these chromatic exercises throughout your vocal range, as is demonstrated on the tracks, your intonation will improve.

Why sing exercises with lyrics?

Lyrics are made up of syllables: vowels and consonants. These can either help or hinder a vocalist in achieving perfect intonation. And although most vocal exercises are sung using only syllables or only vowels, I decided to write lyrics for these exercises. They're designed to train correct pronunciation for those who are not native English speakers, and to habituate clear diction for everyone. They also make it easier to negotiate the transition areas, or "passaggi," between vocal registers,. Some are about music, some are positive thoughts, and some are just for fun, but all have a technical purpose. After mastering these, feel free to get creative and make up your own words or syllables to practice with. Let's explore the sound of this new scale in the following exercises.

You'll hear a slowly sung example before some of the tracks. Enjoy!

In this exercise, you'll sing every ascending interval from the root up to the octave, gradually increasing the intervals by half steps. Then starting on the octave above, you'll sing every descending interval from a half step to the octave below. "Doo" is a good syllable for focusing the tone and checking the tuning. Try this routine in several neighboring keys.

6

Chromatic Intervals with Doo

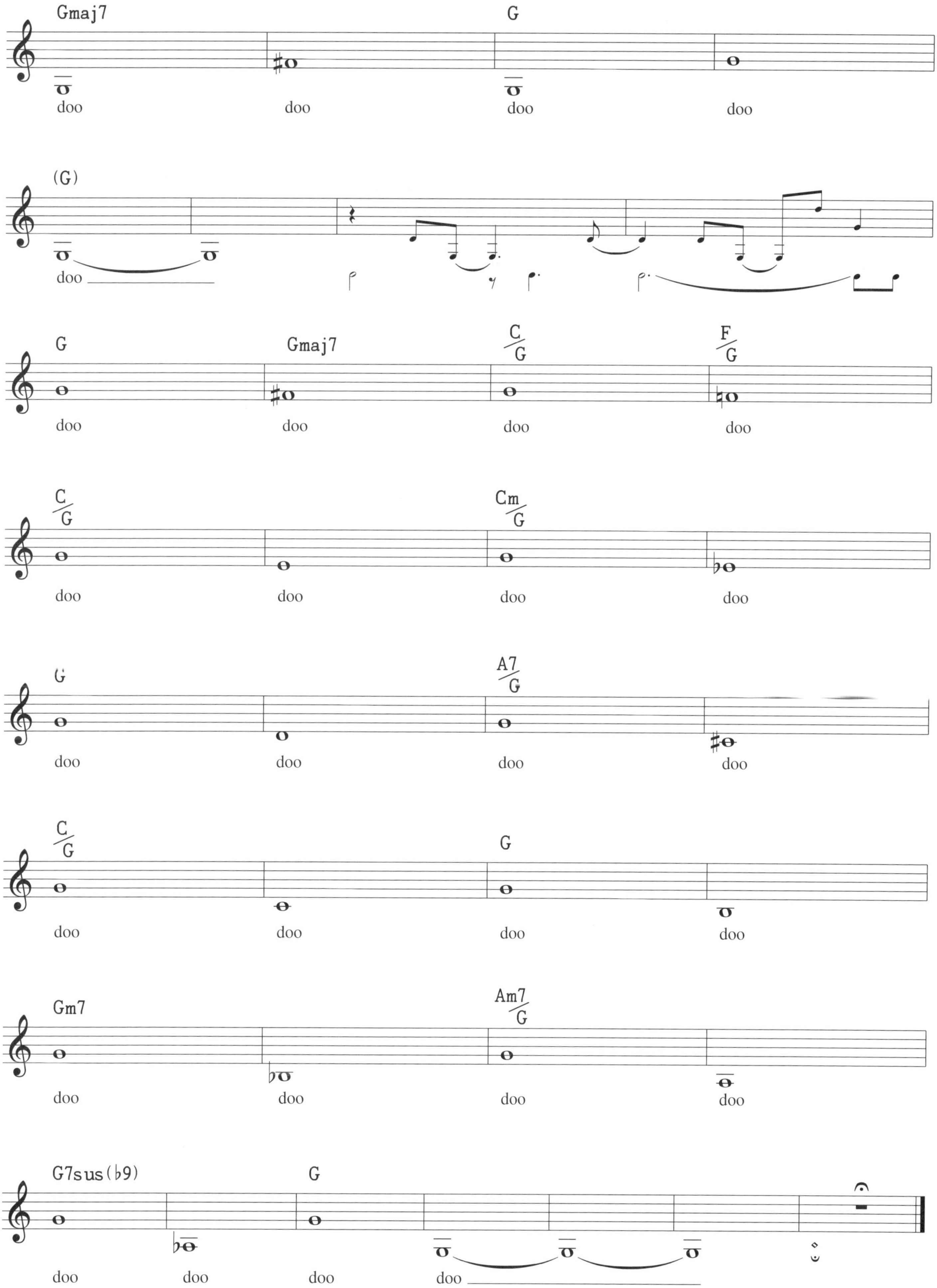
Gmaj7
G
doo doo doo doo
(G)
doo
G
Gmaj7
C/G
F/G
doo doo doo doo
C/G
Cm/G
doo doo doo doo
G
A7/G
doo doo doo doo
C/G
G
doo doo doo doo
Gm7
Am7/G
doo doo doo doo
G7sus(♭9)
G
doo doo doo doo

Now try the same exercise with solfège syllables from the "Moveable Do" system. Just hear it and sing it!

7

Chromatic Intervals Using Solfege Syllables

JUDY NIEMACK

G6
Piano
D/G
C/G
Fmaj7/G
Do Do Ti Do Te
C/G
Cm/G
G(add9)
A7/G
Do La Do Le Do Sol Do Se
C/G
G(add9)
Gm9
C6/G
Do Fa Do Mi Do Me Do Re
G7sus(♭9)
(G)
Do Ra Do Do

As you sing along with this track you'll learn the names of each interval in an octave. The first note is called the "root": the pitch that established the tonality of a musical key, chord, or scale.

8

Chromatic Intervals with Interval Names

Medium even 8ths (♩ = *ca.* 120)

JUDY NIEMACK

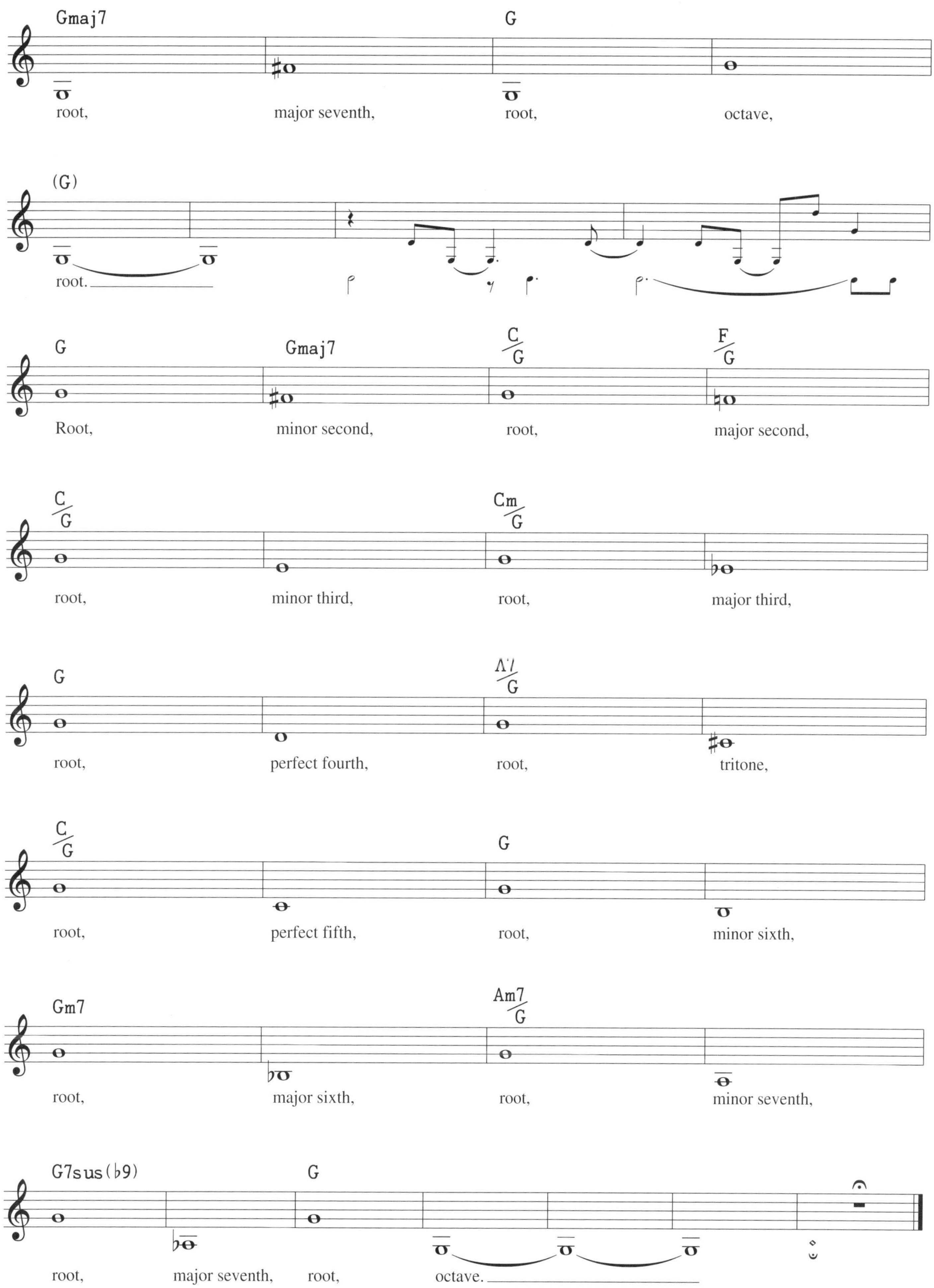
Gmaj7
root,
major seventh,
G
root,
octave,
(G)
root.
G
Root,
Gmaj7
minor second,
C/G
root,
F/G
major second,
C/G
root,
minor third,
Cm/G
root,
major third,
G
root,
perfect fourth,
G
root,
tritone,
C/G
root,
perfect fifth,
G
root,
minor sixth,
Gm7
root,
major sixth,
Am7/G
root,
minor seventh,
G7sus(♭9)
root,
major seventh,
G
root,
octave.

This warm-up will get your voice in gear while teaching you the sound of the Aeolian minor scale. You'll start with a 1-3-5 arpeggio and gradually add notes until you're singing the entire scale. Inhale with the mouth and throat shaped for "ooh" and land gently on the first note, like a feather landing on water.

Aeolian Ooh ah

JUDY NIEMACK

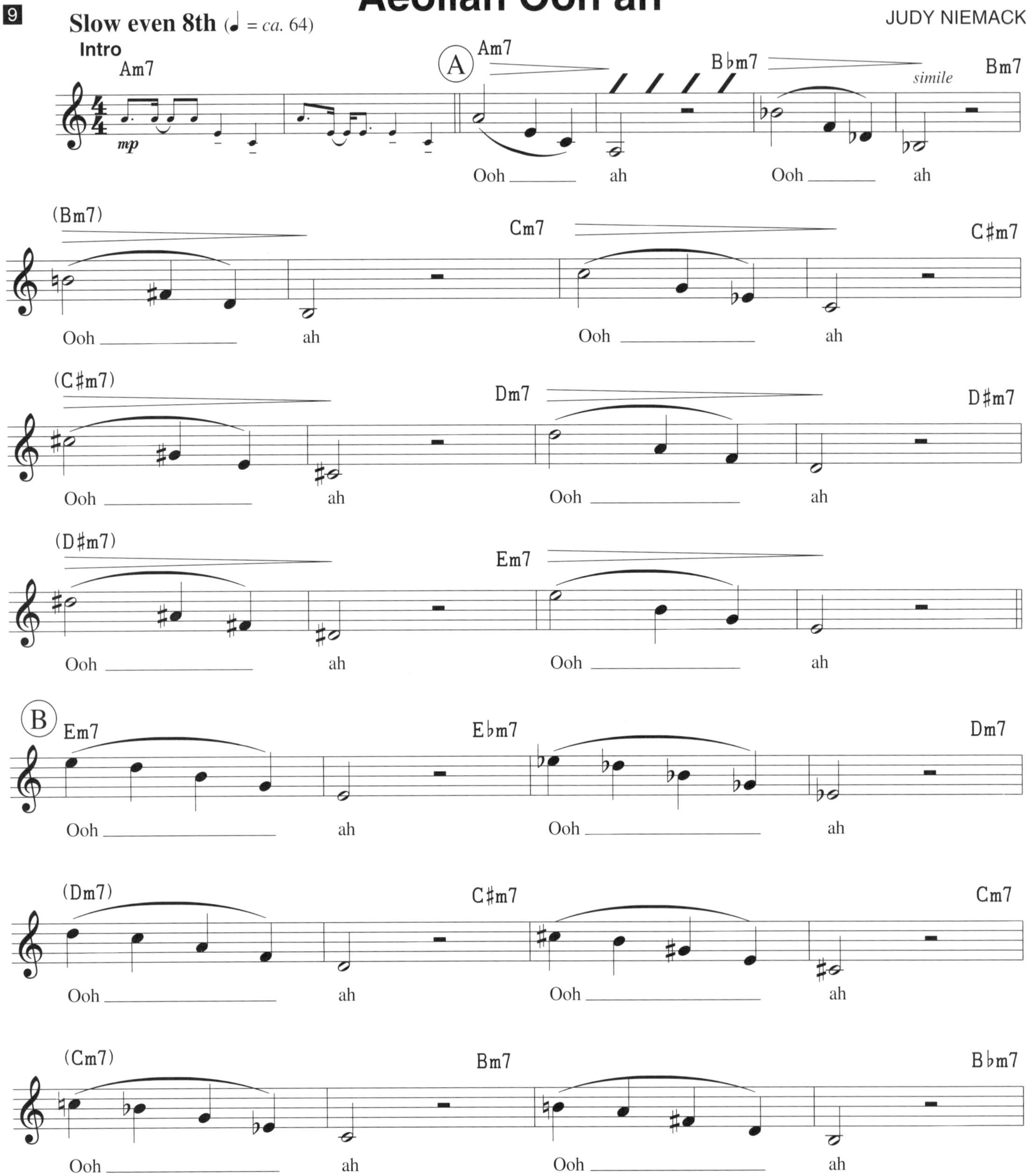

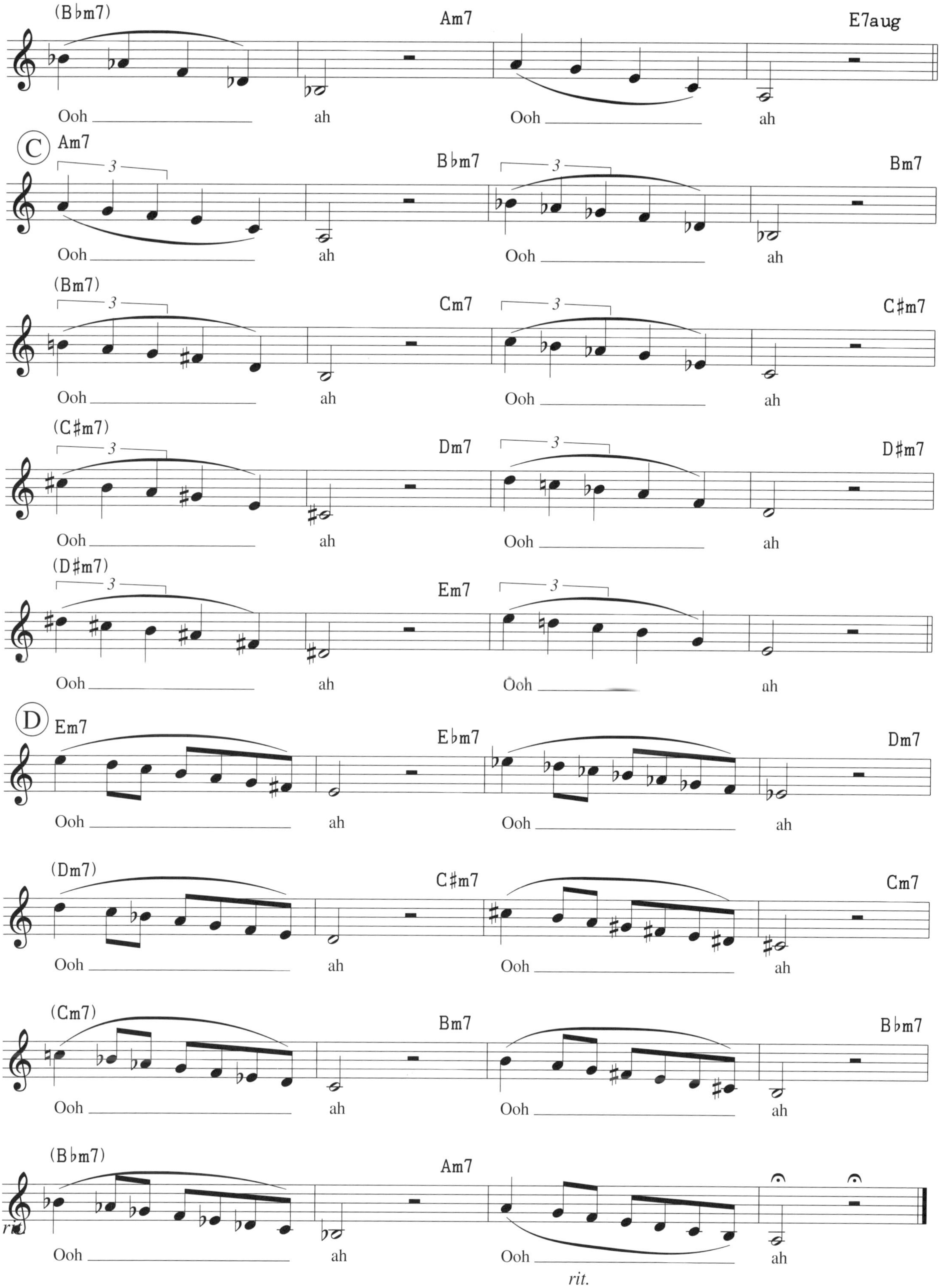
(B♭m7)
Am7
E7aug
Ooh ah Ooh ah
C
Am7
B♭m7
Bm7
Ooh ah Ooh ah
(Bm7)
Cm7
C♯m7
Ooh ah Ooh ah
(C♯m7)
Dm7
D♯m7
Ooh ah Ooh ah
(D♯m7)
Em7
Ooh ah Ooh ah
D
Em7
E♭m7
Dm7
Ooh ah Ooh ah
(Dm7)
C♯m7
Cm7
Ooh ah Ooh ah
(Cm7)
Bm7
B♭m7
Ooh ah Ooh ah
(B♭m7)
Am7
Ooh ah Ooh ah
rit.

This exercise will help smooth out transitions or breaks between vocal registers. By the way, to "croon" is to sing in a soft, soothing voice.

10 Example
11
12

Chromatic Workout: Minor Second

C7 G7♭5 C7
We do swing!
B
G9sus G7(♭9) C6(9)
We're in tune,
F♯9sus F♯7(♭9) B6(9)
while we croon.
F9sus F7(♭9) B♭6(9)
We're in tune,
E9sus E7(♭9) A6(9)
while we croon.
E♭9sus E♭7(♭9) A♭6(9)
We're in tune,
D9sus D7(♭9) G6(9)
while we croon.
D♭9sus D♭7(♭9) G♭6(9)
We're in tune,
C9sus C7(♭9) F6(9)
while we croon.
B9sus B7(♭9) E6(9)
We're in tune,
B♭9sus B♭7(♭9) E♭6(9)
while we croon.
A9sus A7(♭9) D6(9)
We're in tune,
A♭9sus A♭7(♭9) D♭6(9)
while we croon.
G9sus G7(♭9) C6(9)
We're in tune.
Piano
8va

Now you'll sing up and down two half steps: a whole step or Major Second interval. Be sure to accent the upbeats on "la-zy" and "cra-zy."

13 Example
14
15

Chromatic Workout: Major Second

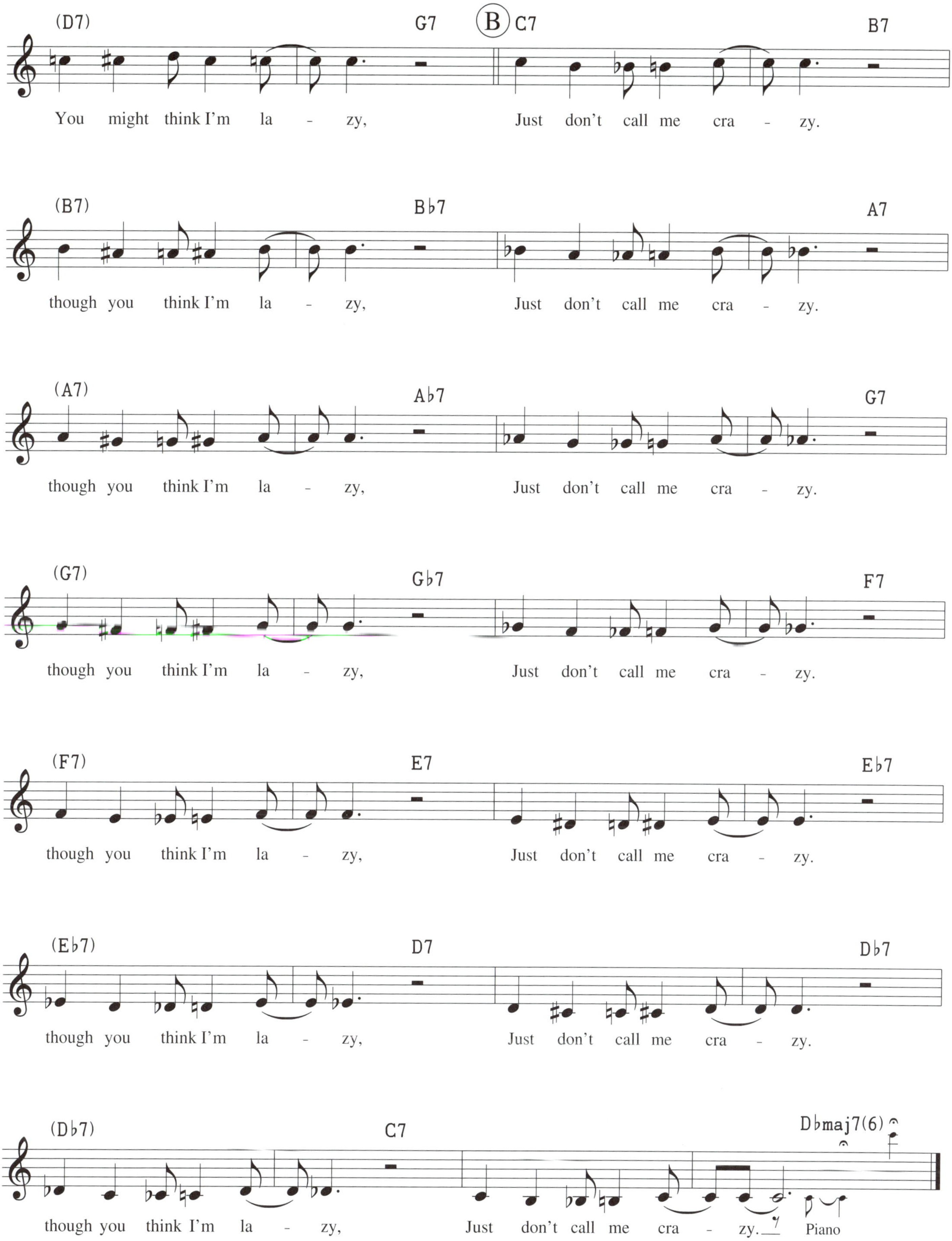
(D7) G7 B C7 B7
You might think I'm la - zy, Just don't call me cra - zy.
(B7) B♭7 A7
though you think I'm la - zy, Just don't call me cra - zy.
(A7) A♭7 G7
though you think I'm la - zy, Just don't call me cra - zy.
(G7) G♭7 F7
though you think I'm la - zy, Just don't call me cra - zy.
(F7) E7 E♭7
though you think I'm la - zy, Just don't call me cra - zy.
(E♭7) D7 D♭7
though you think I'm la - zy, Just don't call me cra - zy.
(D♭7) C7 D♭maj7(6)
though you think I'm la - zy, Just don't call me cra - zy.
Piano

This exercise has the "ooh" vowel on the highest note. The more closed position of the lips helps us to hear ourselves better and to focus the pitch. Again think of smaller half steps as you descend.

16 Example
17
18

Chromatic Workout: Minor Third

Medium swing (♩ = *ca.* 110)

JUDY NIEMACK

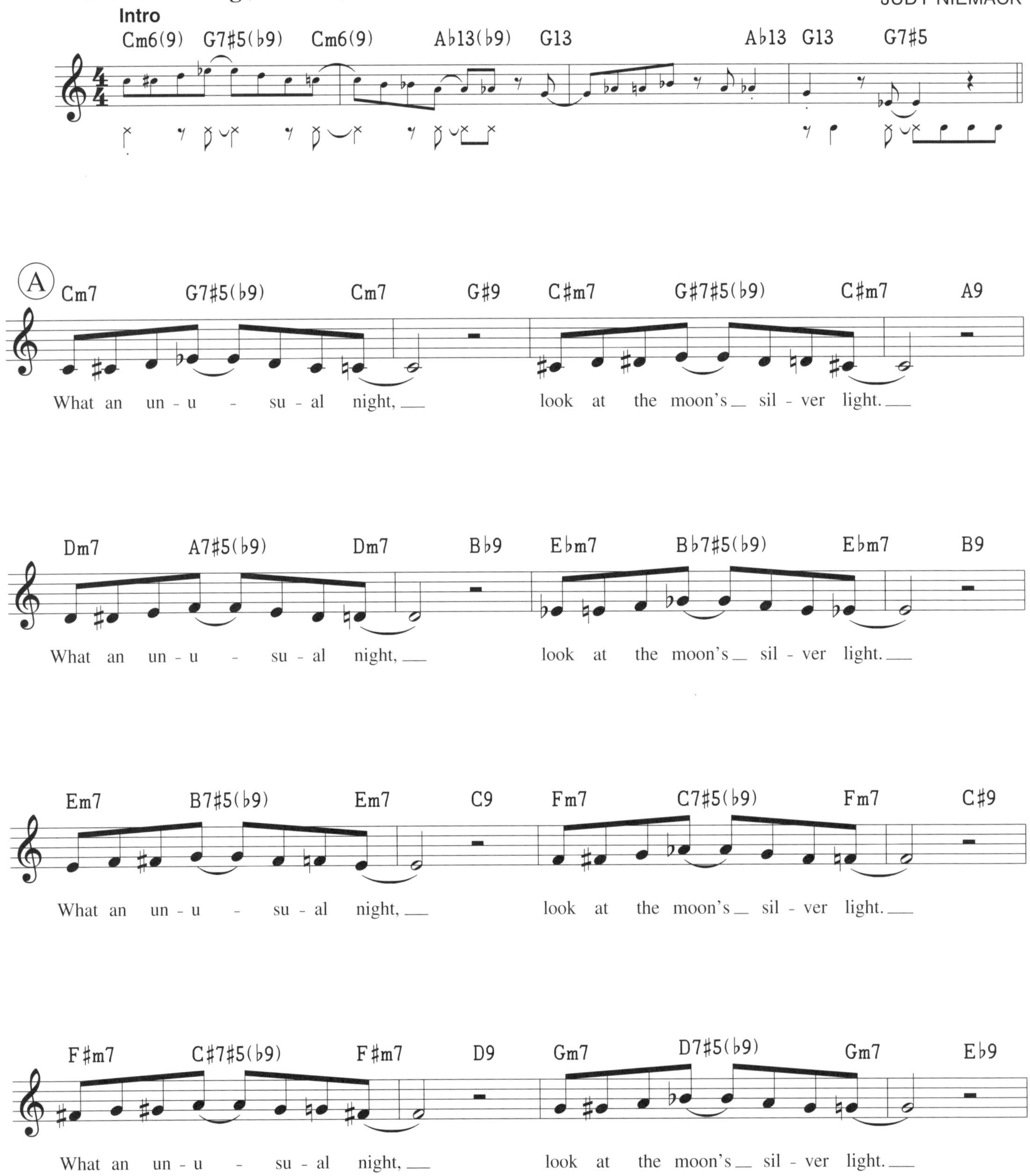

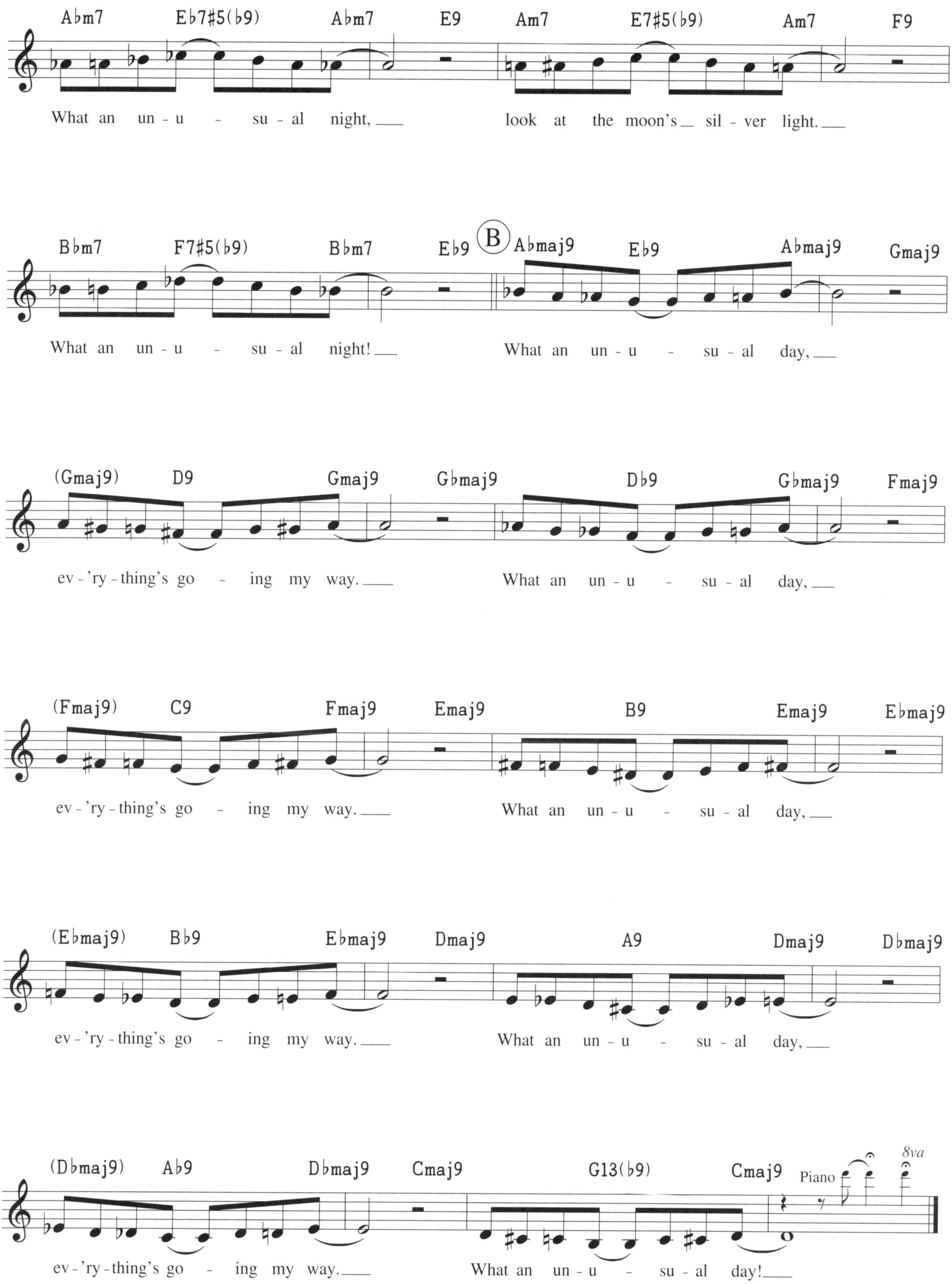
Abm7 Eb7#5(b9) Abm7 E9 Am7 E7#5(b9) Am7 F9
What an un - u - su - al night, look at the moon's sil - ver light.
Bbm7 F7#5(b9) Bbm7 Eb9
What an un - u - su - al night!
B
Abmaj9 Eb9 Abmaj9 Gmaj9
What an un - u - su - al day,
(Gmaj9) D9 Gmaj9 Gbmaj9 Db9 Gbmaj9 Fmaj9
ev - 'ry - thing's go - ing my way. What an un - u - su - al day,
(Fmaj9) C9 Fmaj9 Emaj9 B9 Emaj9 Ebmaj9
ev - 'ry - thing's go - ing my way. What an un - u - su - al day,
(Ebmaj9) Bb9 Ebmaj9 Dmaj9 A9 Dmaj9 Dbmaj9
ev - 'ry - thing's go - ing my way. What an un - u - su - al day,
(Dbmaj9) Ab9 Dbmaj9 Cmaj9 G13(b9) Cmaj9
ev - 'ry - thing's go - ing my way. What an un - u - su - al day!
Piano
8va

Who wouldn't like to float like a feather on a breeze? This exercise gives the lips a good work out if you "chew the words."

19 Example
20
21

Chromatic Workout: Major Third

Medium slow Latin (♩ = *ca.* 88)

JUDY NIEMACK

Intro

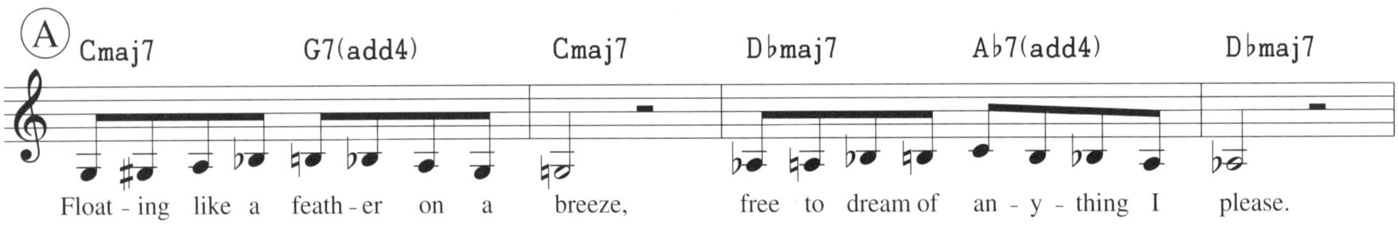

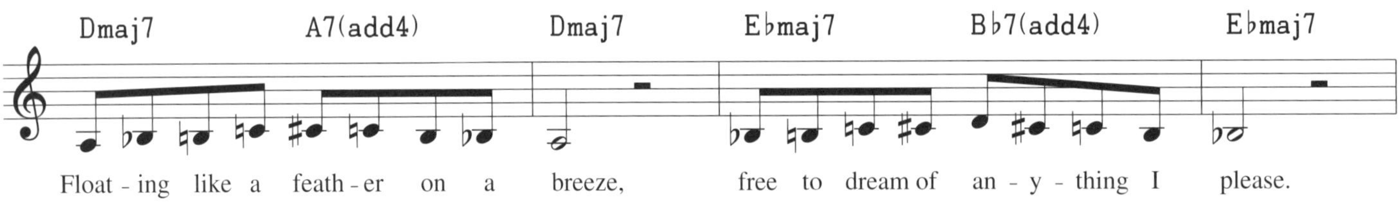

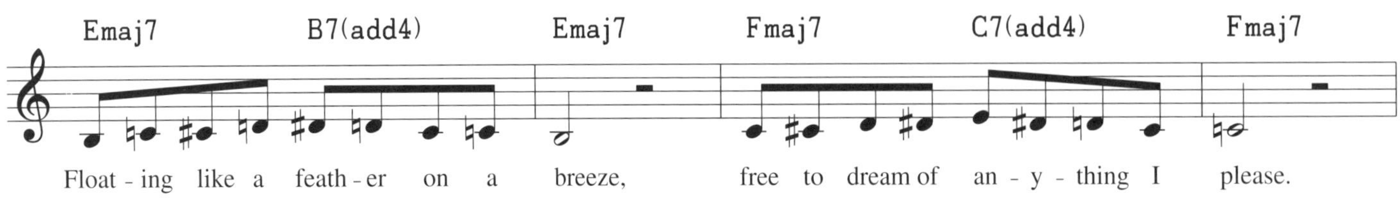

Gbmaj7 Db7(add4) Gbmaj7 Gmaj7 D7(add4) Gmaj7
Float - ing like a feath - er on a breeze, free to dream of an - y - thing I please.
Abmaj7 Eb7(add4) Abmaj7 Amaj7 E7(add4) Amaj7
Float - ing like a feath - er on a breeze, free to dream of an - y - thing I please.
Bbmaj7 F7(add4) Bbmaj7 Bmaj7 F#7(add4) Bmaj7
Float - ing like a feath - er on a breeze, free to dream of an - y - thing I please.
G13sus
rit.
C6(9)
Piano
Free to dream of an - y - thing I please.

Pay attention to the tuning on the first syllables of "with-in" and "be-gin" to be sure they're high enough. For female voices, as the exercise ascends, you may notice a "flip" or "break" in your sound. Resist the urge to push the lower register up. If you lighten your breath pressure, the vocal mechanism will adjust smoothly as you enter the higher register.

22 Example
23
24

Chromatic Workout: Perfect Fourth

Medium slow Latin (♩ = *ca.* 94)

JUDY NIEMACK

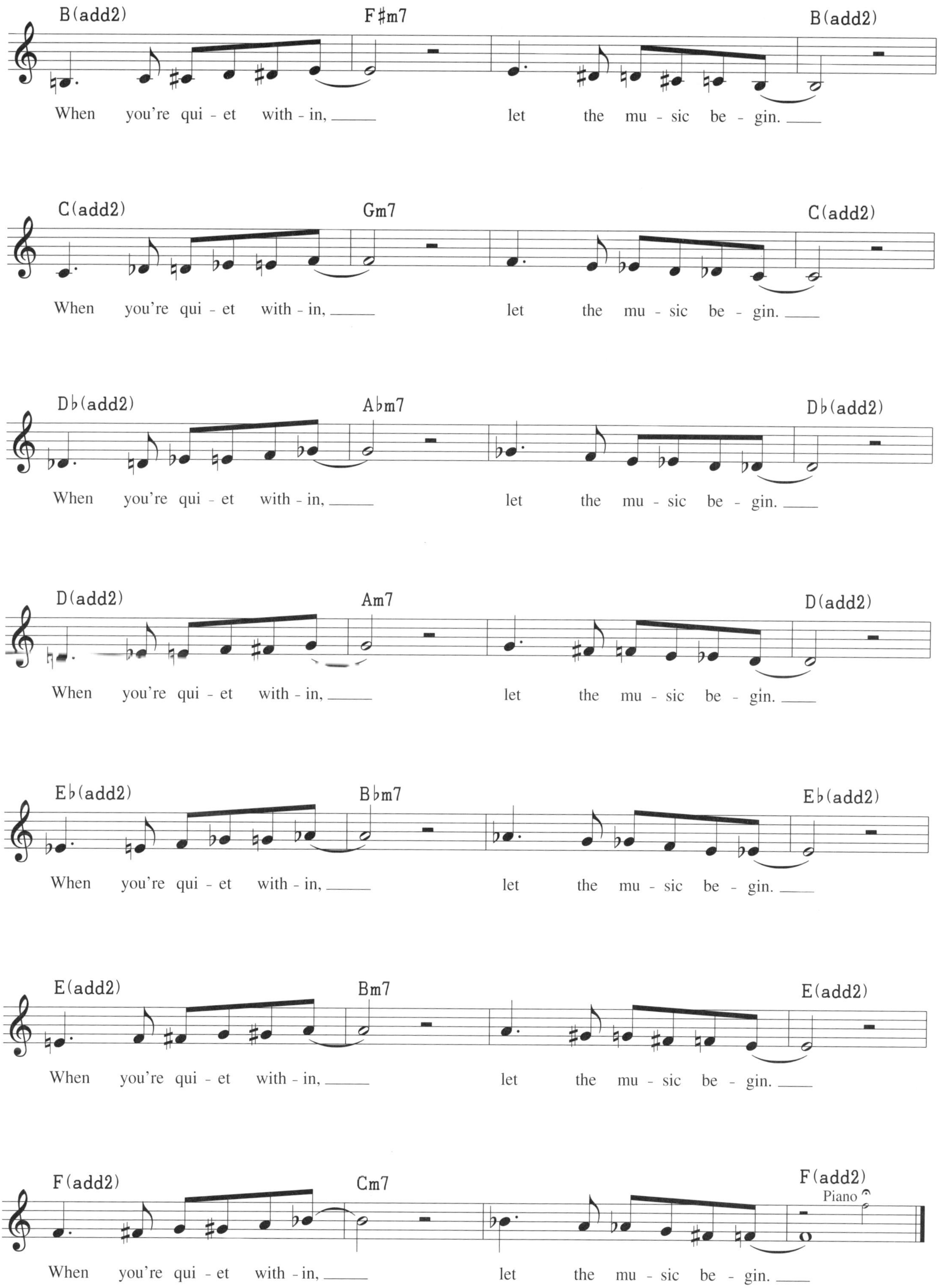
B(add2)
F♯m7
B(add2)
When you're qui - et with - in, let the mu - sic be - gin.
C(add2)
Gm7
C(add2)
When you're qui - et with - in, let the mu - sic be - gin.
D♭(add2)
A♭m7
D♭(add2)
When you're qui - et with - in, let the mu - sic be - gin.
D(add2)
Am7
D(add2)
When you're qui - et with - in, let the mu - sic be - gin.
E♭(add2)
B♭m7
E♭(add2)
When you're qui - et with - in, let the mu - sic be - gin.
E(add2)
Bm7
E(add2)
When you're qui - et with - in, let the mu - sic be - gin.
F(add2)
Cm7
F(add2)
Piano
When you're qui - et with - in, let the mu - sic be - gin.

This melody emphasizes the augmented fourth degree of the scale. The first phrase ends on the augmented fourth with "play," and the second phrase starts with it on "all." Enjoy this dissonant, beautiful color.

25 Example

26

27

Chromatic Workout: Augmented Fourth

Medium Latin (♩ = *ca.* 124)

JUDY NIEMACK

In this exercise, try giving more emphasis to the upbeats: "Won't you take a jour-ney with me." This will improve your intonation

28 Example

29

30

Chromatic Workout: Perfect Fifth

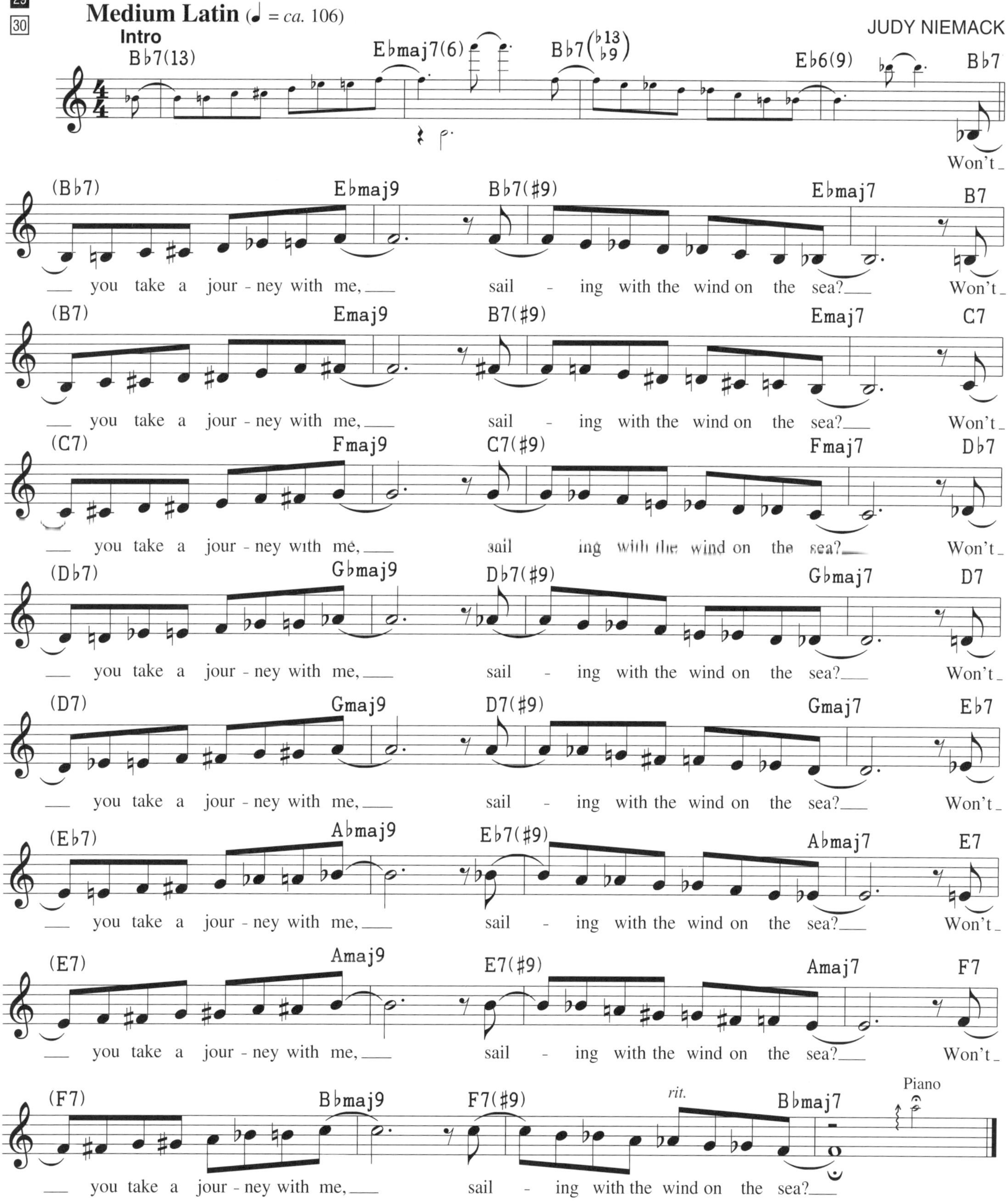

When ascending chromatically, tune up "dan-cing" and "have" by imagining the half steps as slightly larger. When singing a descending line, as in "while the mu-sic car-ries you away," try thinking of the half steps as slightly smaller.

31 Example
32
33

Chromatic Workout: Minor Sixth

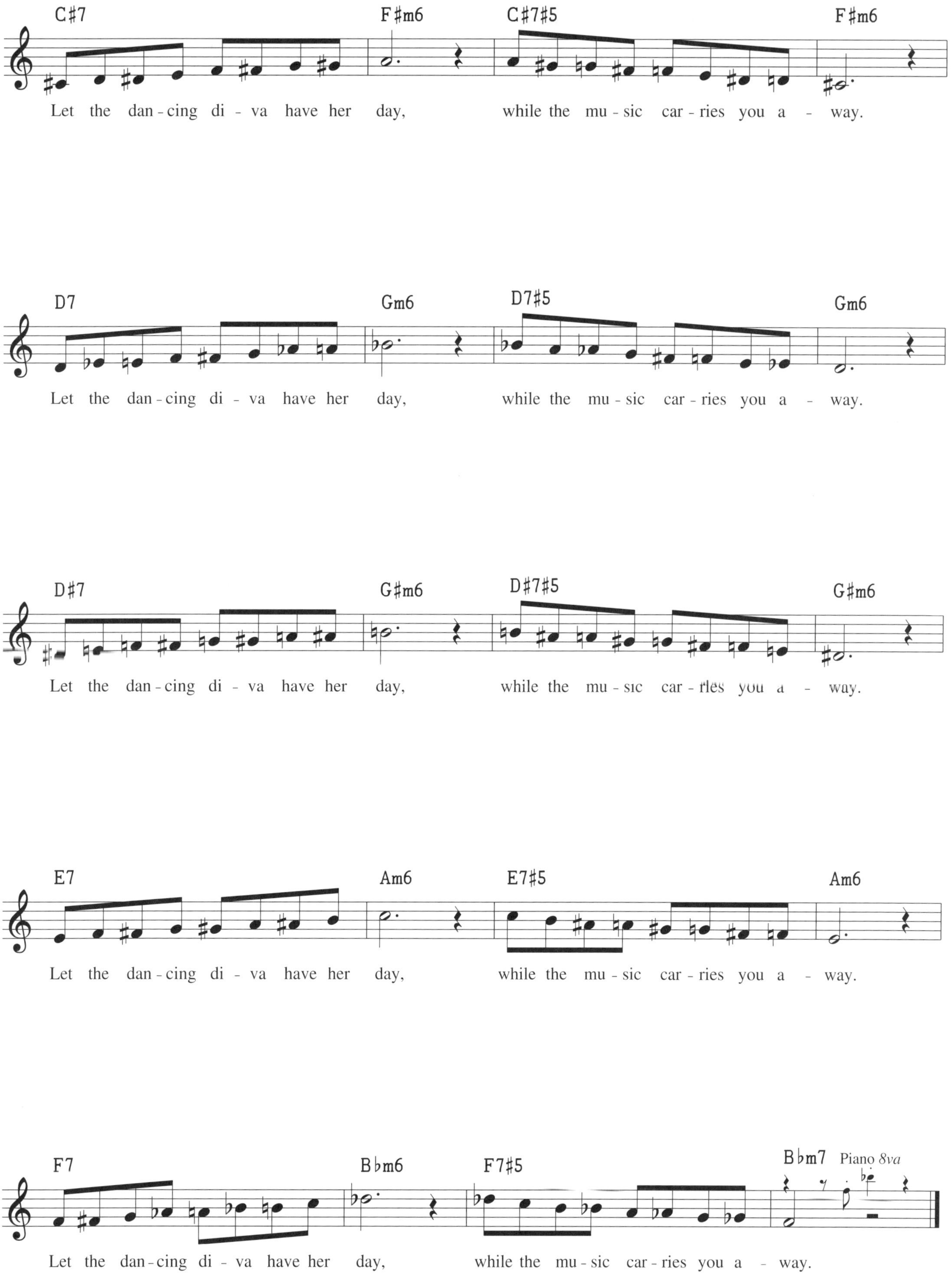
C♯7 F♯m6 C♯7♯5 F♯m6
Let the dan - cing di - va have her day, while the mu - sic car - ries you a - way.
D7 Gm6 D7♯5 Gm6
Let the dan - cing di - va have her day, while the mu - sic car - ries you a - way.
D♯7 G♯m6 D♯7♯5 G♯m6
Let the dan - cing di - va have her day, while the mu - sic car - ries you a - way.
E7 Am6 E7♯5 Am6
Let the dan - cing di - va have her day, while the mu - sic car - ries you a - way.
F7 B♭m6 F7♯5 B♭m7 Piano 8va
Let the dan - cing di - va have her day, while the mu - sic car - ries you a - way.

The first phrase outlines a diminished seventh chord; the second is a chromatic scale from the root up to the Major 6th and down again. Get a good breath: it's a long phrase!

34 Example
35
36

Chromatic Workout: Major Sixth

Slow swing (♩ = *ca.* 64)

JUDY NIEMACK

Cdim7
When I sing di - min - ished chords
I like to sing ev - 'ry note in a row so I know where the next one will go.
Bdim7
When I sing di - min - ished chords
I like to sing ev - 'ry note in a row so I know where the next one will go.
B♭dim7
When I sing di - min - ished chords
I like to sing ev - 'ry note in a row so I know where the next one will go.
Adim7
When I sing di - min - ished chords
I like to sing ev - 'ry note in a row so I know where the next one will go.
G♯dim7
When I sing di - min - ished chords
I like to sing ev - 'ry note in a row so I know where the next one will go.

This exercise requires efficient breath management in order to sing the phrases on one breath. While you're working up to that, breathe where you need to, as long as it makes sense in the sentence. The priority this time is intonation.

37 Example
38
39

Chromatic Workout: Minor Seventh

Medium swing (♩ = *ca.* 118)

JUDY NIEMACK

(C7) B♭7 B7 C7
you want to groove you've got to move your feet! Swing
(C7) C7♭5 D7 G7♭5 C7 D♭7
that rhy - thm now and start to feel that beat. If
(D♭7) B7 C7 D♭7
you want to groove you've got to move your feet! Swing
(D♭7) D♭7♭5 E♭7 A♭7♭5 D♭7 D7
that rhy - thm now and start to feel that beat. If
(D7) C7 D♭7 D7
you want to groove you've got to move your feet! Swing
(D7) D7♭5 E7 A7♭5 D7 E♭7
that rhy - thm now and start to feel that beat. If
(E♭7) D♭7 D7 E♭7
you want to groove you've got to move your feet! Swing
(E♭7) E♭7♭5 F7 B♭7♭5 E♭7
Piano
that rhy - thm now and start to feel that beat.

Here's a melody covering every half step in a major seventh interval. Practice singing it "legato," in a smooth, flowing manner, without any breaks between the notes. On the words "day" and "say," hold the "Eh" sound longer than the "Ee" sound.

40 Example
41
42

Chromatic Workout: Major Seventh

Medium Latin (♩ = *ca.* 100)

JUDY NIEMACK

B7 B7sus E7 B♭7 A F7sus
Walk-in' down the street, I'm look - in' for a sun ray.
Cm7 F7 E♭m7 Dm7 G7sus G7
Spring is in the air, is - n't it a love - ly day?
C7 C7sus F7 B7 B♭ F♯7sus
Walk-in' down the street, I'm look - in' for a sun ray.
C♯m7 F♯7 Em7 D♯m7 G♯7sus G♯7
Spring is in the air, is - n't it a love - ly day?
C♯7 C♯7sus F♯7 C7 B G7sus
Walk-in' down the street, I'm look - in' for a sun ray.
Dm7 G7 Fm7 Em7 A7sus A7
Spring is in the air, is - n't it a love - ly day?
D7 D7sus G7 D♭7 C
Piano
Walk-in' down the street, I'm look - in' for a sun ray.
rit.

Finally, here are all of the notes in a chromatic scale, from the root to the octave. The "oh" vowel is featured in this workout.

43 Example

44

45

Chromatic Workout: Octave

Medium even 8ths (♩ = *ca.* 108)

(Tango)

JUDY NIEMACK

Dm6 Aaug Dm6
Ris- ing from be - low, go - ing with the flow, feel that gold- en glow.
Dm6 Aaug Dm6
Fall - ing down a - gain, ev - 'ry now and then, learn - ing to let go.
E♭m6 B♭aug E♭m6
Ris - ing from be - low, go - ing with the flow, feel that gold- en glow.
E♭m6 B♭aug E♭m6
Fall - ing down a - gain, ev - 'ry now and then, learn - ing to let go.
Em6 Baug Em6
Ris - ing from be - low, go - ing with the flow, feel that gold- en glow.
Em6 Baug Em6
Piano
Fall - ing down a - gain, ev - 'ry now and then, learn - ing to let go.

Section 3: ARPEGGIOS

Here are eight exercises designed to increase your range while training your ear. You'll be singing arpeggiated Major and Dominant 7th chords throughout your range, adding the "color" notes, or "extensions" (9, ♯11, 13), with each subsequent track. As you sing along, you'll exercise your high notes and become more comfortable with the harmonic colors commonly used in jazz. Try using the syllables "See - yoo" on these exercises if the "yah" sound is hard to control.

46

Major Seventh Arpeggios

Medium Latin (♩ = *ca.* 126)

JUDY NIEMACK

Intro

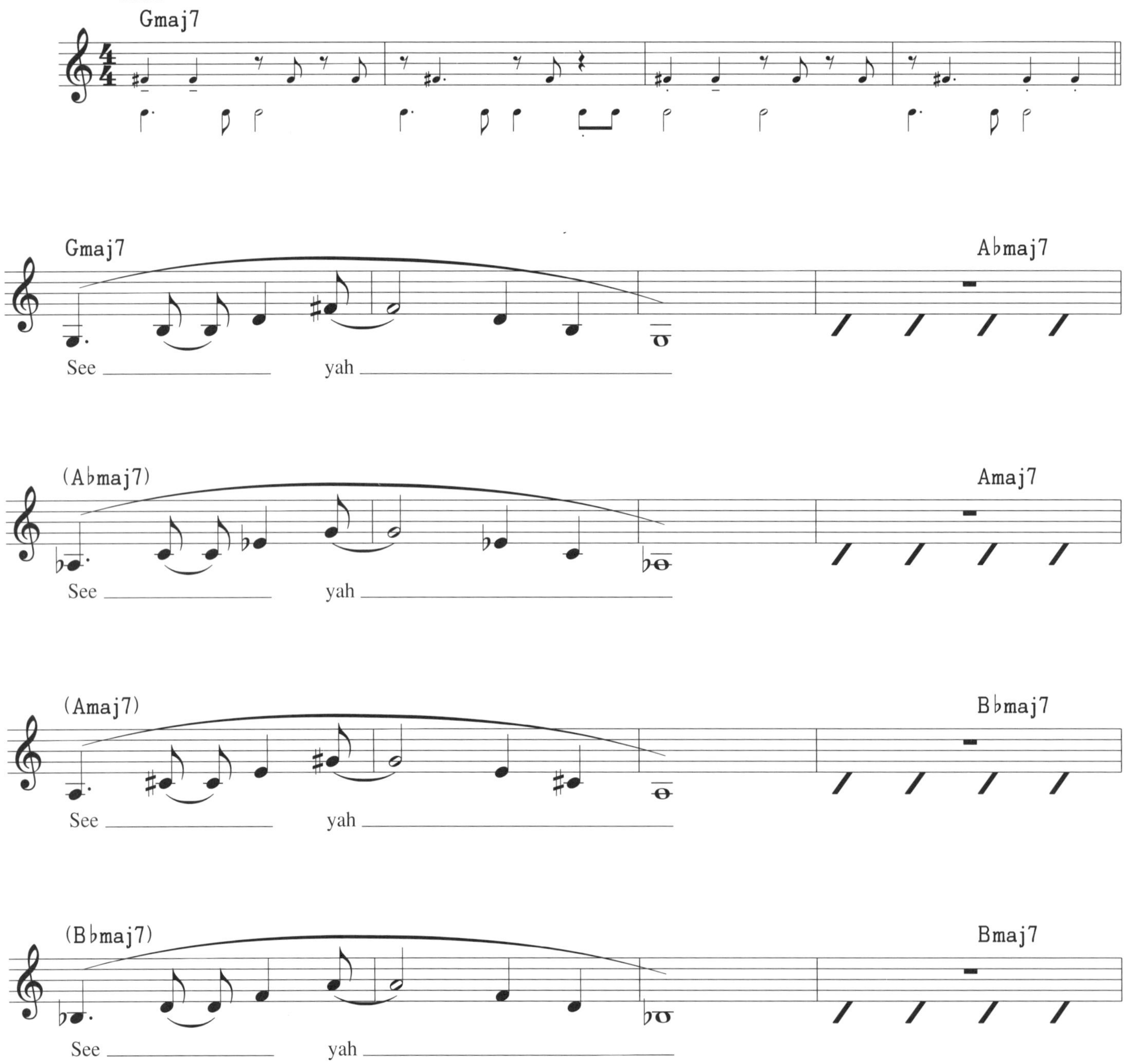

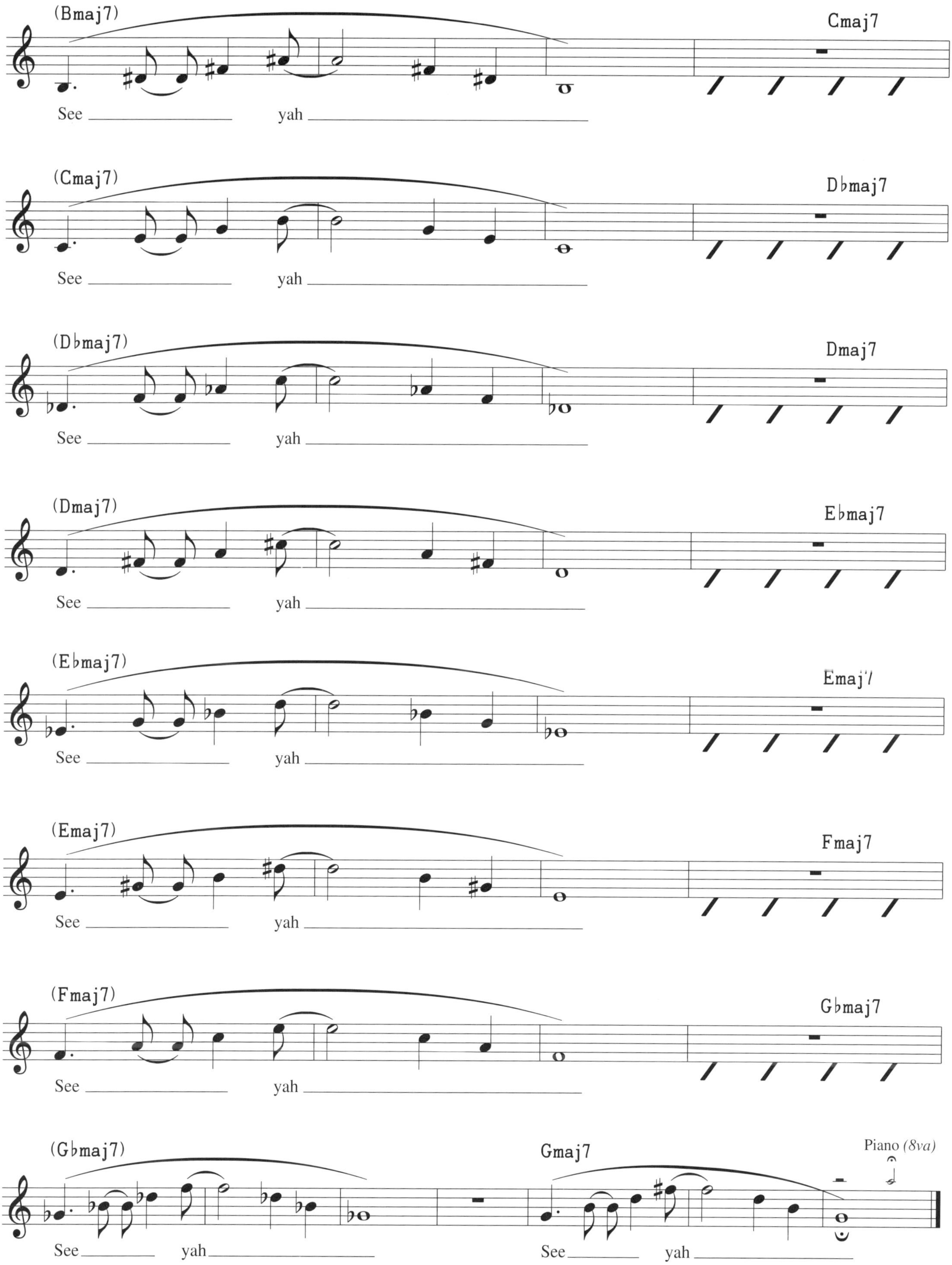
(Bmaj7)
Cmaj7
See
yah
(Cmaj7)
D♭maj7
See
yah
(D♭maj7)
Dmaj7
See
yah
(Dmaj7)
E♭maj7
See
yah
(E♭maj7)
Emaj7
See
yah
(Emaj7)
Fmaj7
See
yah
(Fmaj7)
G♭maj7
See
yah
(G♭maj7)
Gmaj7
Piano (8va)
See
yah
See
yah

47

Major Ninth Arpeggios

Medium Latin (♩ = *ca.* 124)

JUDY NIEMACK

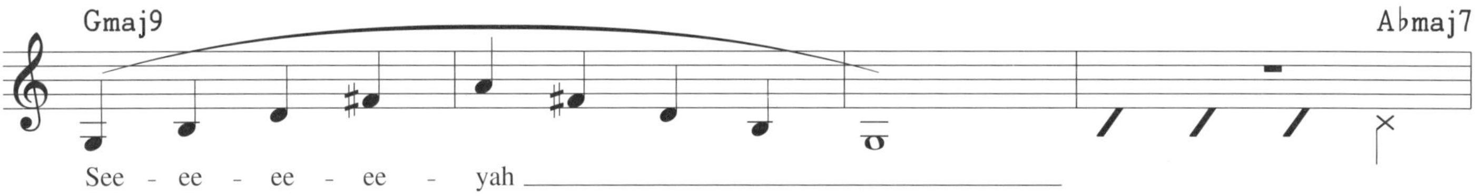

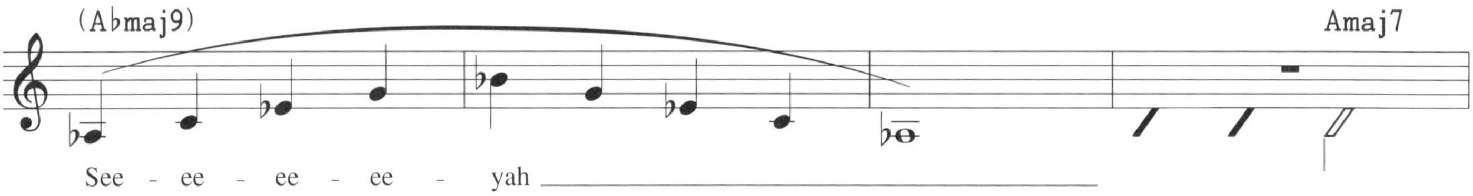

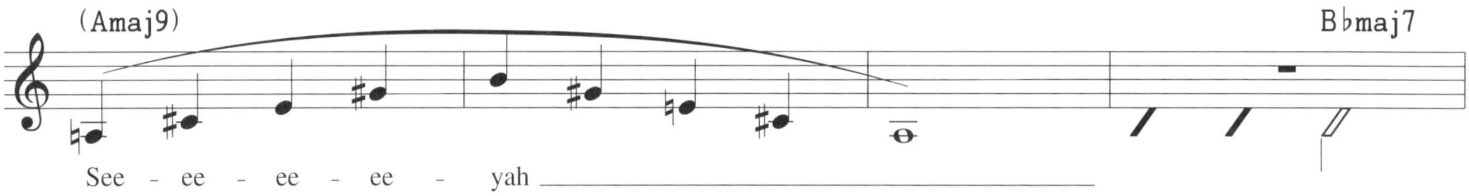

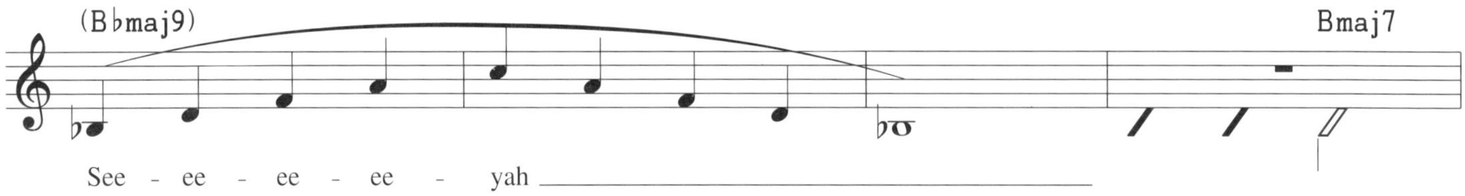

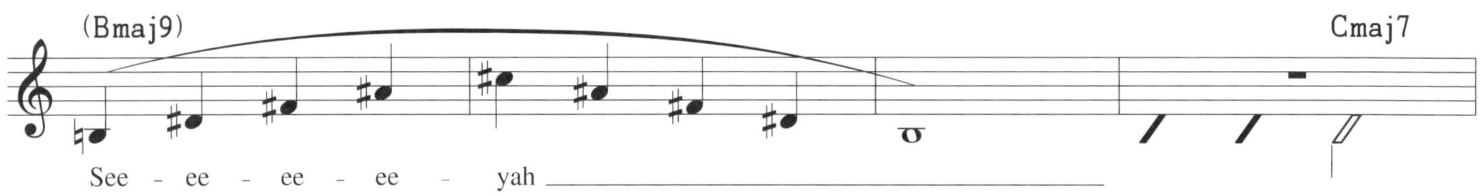

(Cmaj9)
Dbmaj7
See - ee - ee - ee - yah
(Dbmaj9)
Dmaj7
See - ee - ee - ee - yah
(Dmaj9)
Ebmaj7
See - ee - ee - ee - yah
(Ebmaj9)
Emaj7
See - ee - ee - ee - yah
(Emaj9)
Fmaj7
See - ee - ee - ee - yah
(Fmaj9)
Gbmaj9
See - ee - ee - ee - yah
(Gbmaj9)
Gmaj9
See - ee - ee - ee - yah
(Gmaj9)
See - ee - ee - ee - yah
Piano

48

Major Sharp Eleventh Arpeggios

Slow even 8ths (♩ = *ca.* 82)

JUDY NIEMACK

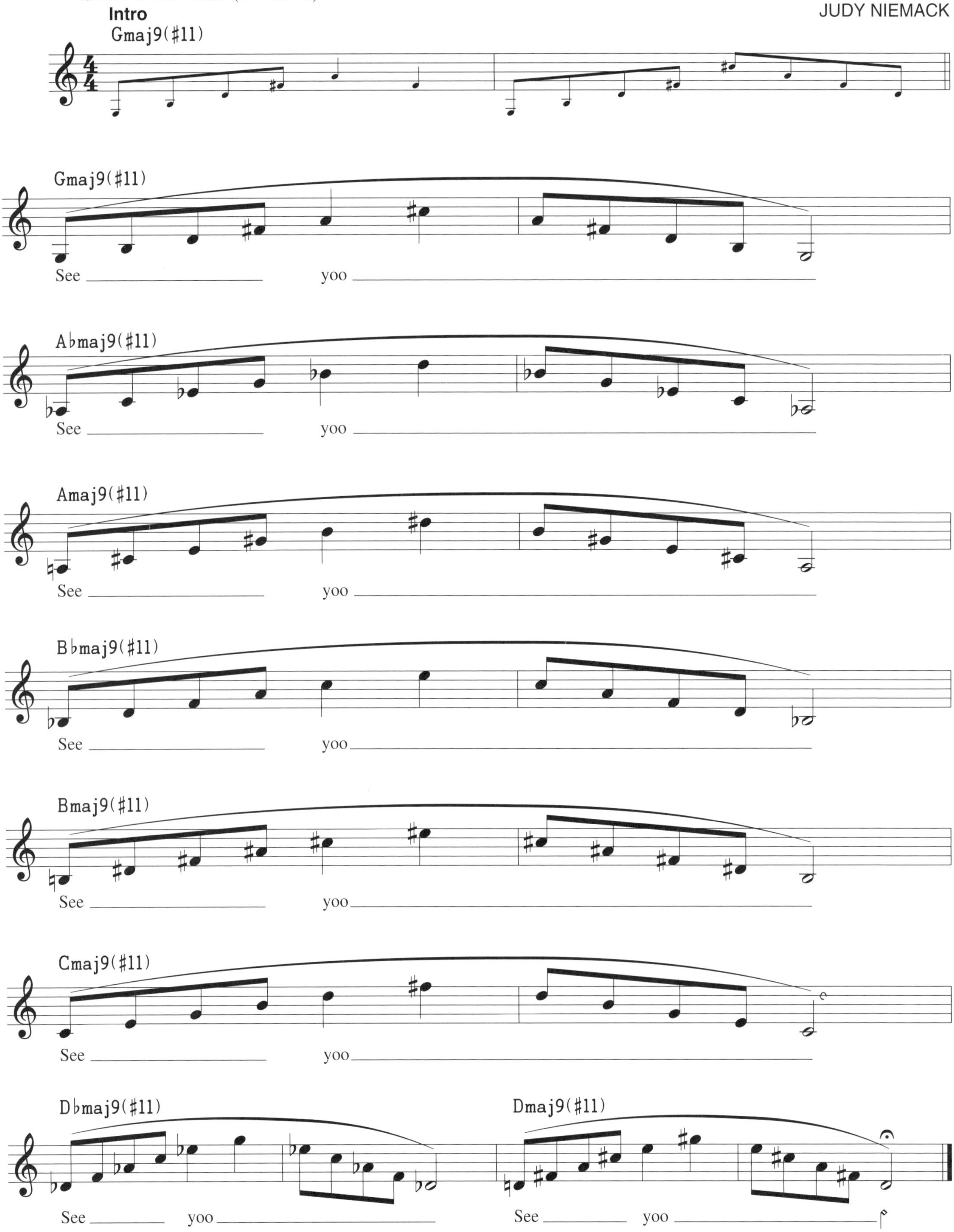

49

Major Thirteenth Arpeggios

JUDY NIEMACK

Slow (♩. = *ca.* 52)

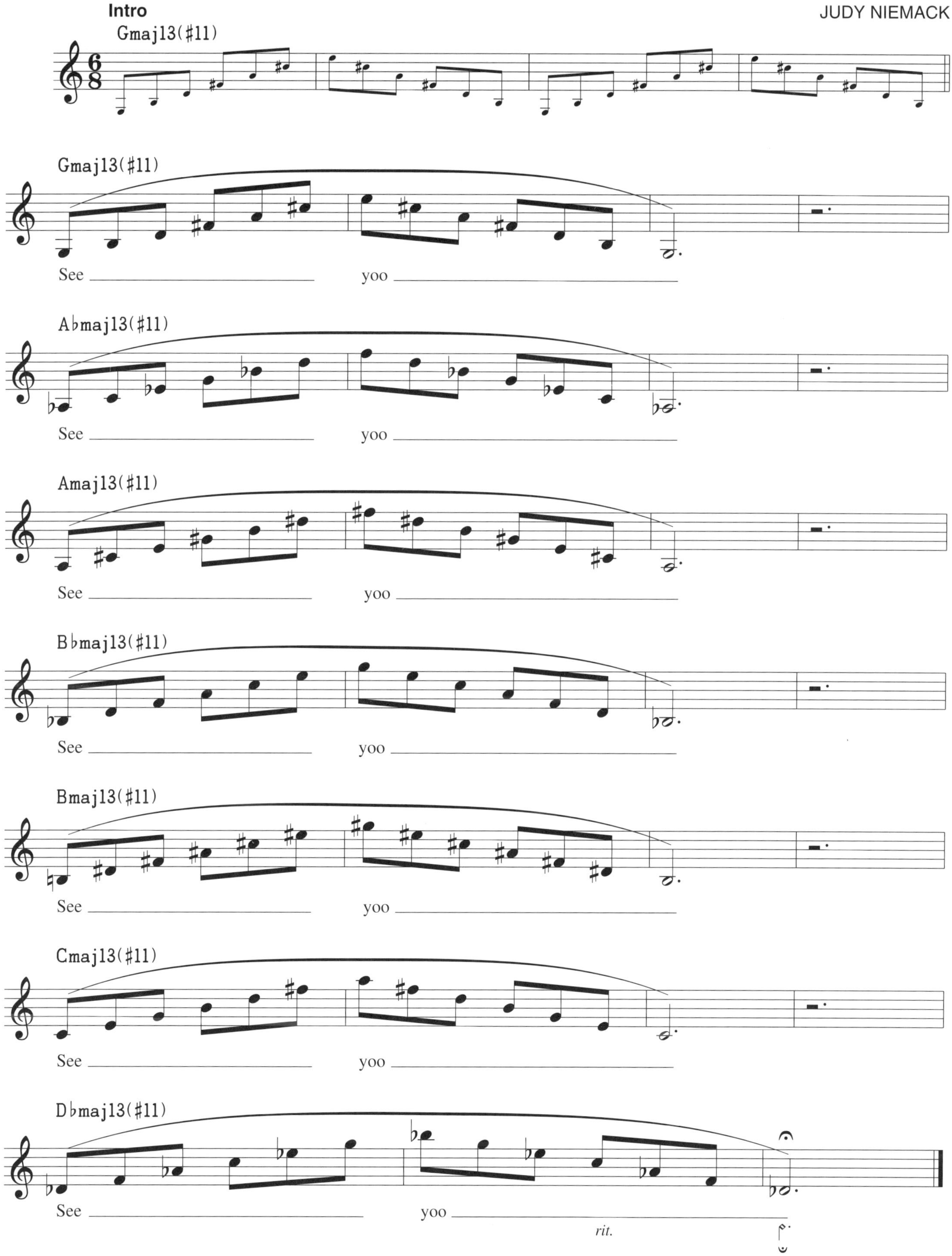

50

Dominant Seventh Arpeggios

Medium even 8ths (♩ = *ca.* 114)

JUDY NIEMACK

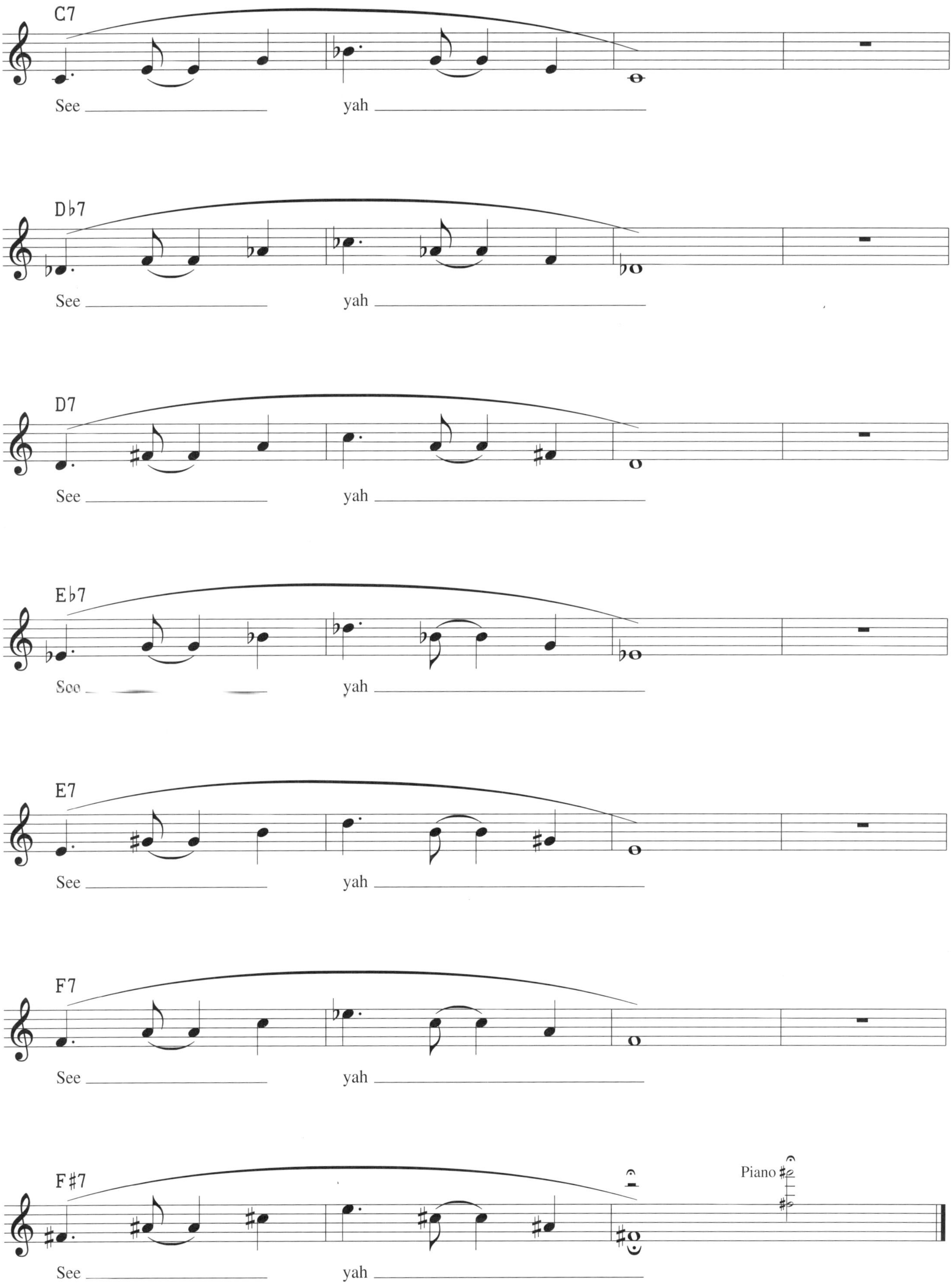
C7
See
yah
D♭7
See
yah
D7
See
yah
E♭7
See
yah
E7
See
yah
F7
See
yah
F♯7
See
yah
Piano

51

Dominant Ninth Arpeggios

Medium even 8ths (♩ = *ca.* 132) JUDY NIEMACK

D♭9
Da ba - da - ba ba ___ ya da - da - da
D9
Da ba - da - ba ba ___ ya da - da - da
E♭9
Da ba - da - ba ba ___ ya da - da - da
E9
Da ba - da - ba ba ___ ya da - da - da
F9
Da ba - da - ba ba ___ ya da - da - da
F♯9
Da ba - da - ba ba ___ ya da - da - da
G9
Piano
Da ba - da - ba ba ___ ya da - da - da

52

Dominant Sharp Eleventh Arpeggios

Medium even 8ths (♩ = *ca.* 116)

JUDY NIEMACK

Intro

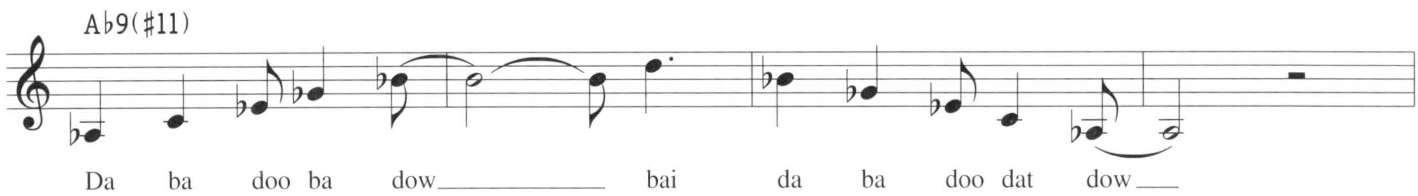

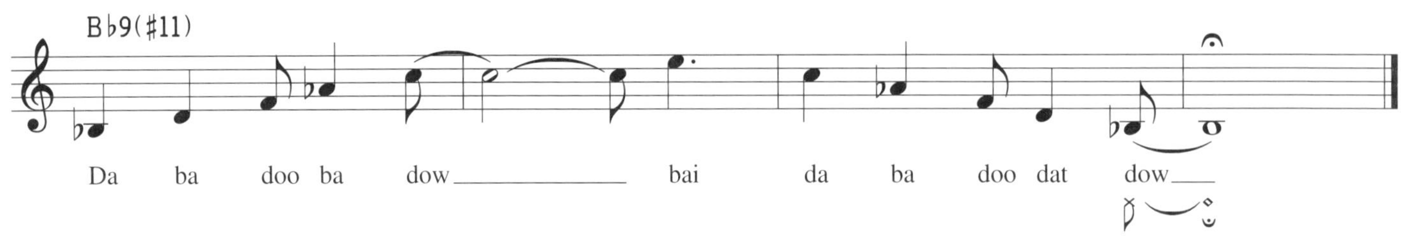

53

Dominant Thirteenth Arpeggios

Medium slow (♩. = *ca.* 58)   JUDY NIEMACK

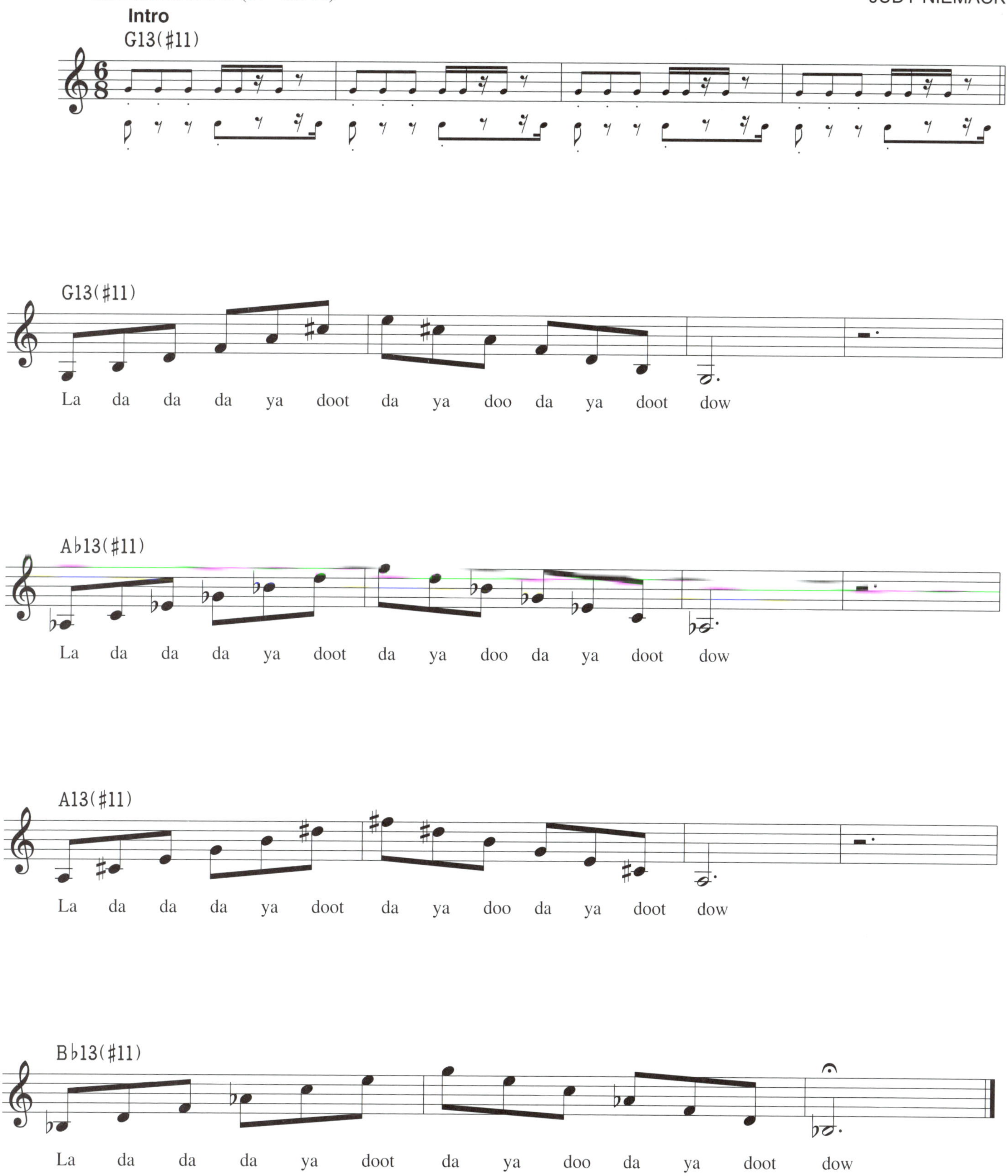

Examples from the Repertoire

There are many beautiful songs with chromatic passages or chromatic approach notes. As an exercise to develop pitch accuracy, find the chromatic phrases in these songs and practice them throughout your range, moving them up and down in half steps.

Vocal Jazz Standards with chromatic passages

April in Paris (Vernon Duke)
The Best is Yet to Come (Cy Coleman, Carolyn Leigh)
Blue and Sentimental (Count Basie, Mel Torme)
Born to be Blue (Mel Tormé, Robert Wells)
Boulevard of Broken Dreams (Al Dubin, Harry Warren)
Boy Next Door (Hugh Martin, Ralph Blane)
Darn that Dream (Jimmy Van Heusen, Eddie De Lange)
Don't Get Around Much Anymore (Duke Ellington, Bob Russell)
Early Autumn (Ralph Burns, Johnny Mercer)
Easy Living (Ralph Rainger, Leo Robin)
Caravan (Duke Ellington, Juan Tizol, Irving Mills)
Sophisticated Lady (Duke Ellington, Irving Mills, Mitchell Parish)
Prelude to a Kiss (Duke Ellington, Irving Gordon, Irving Mills)
Lush Life (Billy Strayhorn)
Do Nothing 'Til You Hear From Me (Duke Ellington, Bob Russell)
A Flower is a Lovesome Thing (Billy Strayhorn)
Get It Straight (a/k/a: "Straight No Chaser") (Thelonious Monk, Sally Swisher)
Heart's Desire (Alan Broadbent, Dave Frishberg)
I Concentrate on You (Cole Porter)
I've Got You Under My Skin (Cole Porter)
If I Had You (Irving King, Ted Shapiro)
Just in Time (Jules Styne, Betty Comden, Adolph Green)
Last Night When We Were Young (Harold Arlen, Yip Harburg)
Lover (Richard Rogers, Lorenz Hart)
Lucky to Be Me (Leonard Bernstein)
Mean to Me (Fred Ahlert, Roy Turk)
Midnight Sun (John Francis Burke, Johnny Mercer)
Monkery's the Blues (a/k/a: "Blue Monk") (Thelonious Monk, Abbey Lincoln)
Once Upon a Summertime (Johnny Mercer, Michel Legrand, Eddie Barclay, Eddy Marnay)
Only the Lonely (Sammy Cahn, James Van Heusen)
Poor Butterfly (John Golden, Raymond Hubbell)
A Timeless Place (a/k/a: "The Peacocks") (Jimmy Rowles, Norma Winstone)
When I look in Your Eyes (Leslie Bricusse)

White Christmas (Irving Berlin)
Winter in Madrid (Gene Roland , Jacques Cascales)
Withcraft (Cy Coleman, Carolyn Leigh)
Yesterdays (Jerome Kern, Otto Harbach)
You and the Night and the Music (Arthur Schwartz, Howard Dietz)
You've Changed (Carl Fischer, William Carey)

Instrumental Jazz
Chelsea Bridge (Billy Strayhorn)
Hot House (Tadd Dameron)
Lester Left Town (Wayne Shorter)
Lotus Blossum (Billy Strayhorn)
Nuages (Django Reinhart)
The Alley Cat Song (Bent Fabricius-Bjerre)
The Mooche (Duke Ellington, Irving Mills)

Pop Songs
Don't You Worry `bout a Thing (Stevie Wonder)
Sir Duke (Stevie Wonder)

Brazilian Songs
Eu te Amo (Chico Buarque)
Insensatez (A.C. Jobim)
Inutil Passagem (A.C Jobim)
Luisa (A.C. Jobim)
Retrato im Branco y Preto (aka: "Zingaro") (A.C. Jobim)
Watch What Happens (Michel Legrand)

Well-known classical music
La Habañera from "Carmen" (Georges Bizet)
Etude Opus 10, no.2 (Frédéric Chopin)
Prelude in Em, Opus 28 no.4 (Frédéric Chopin)
Entry of the Gladiators (Julius Fuçik)
Tango Jalousi (Jacob Gade)
Rhapsody in Blue George (Gershwin)
Grand Galop Chromatique (Franz Liszt)
Intermezzo from "Cavalleria Rusticana" (Pietro Mascagni)
String Quartet No. 16 in Eb Major (Wolfgang Amadeus Mozart)
Flight of the Bumblebee (Nikolai Rimsky-Korsakov)
Song of the Evening Star from "Tannhäuser" (Richard Wagner)

About Judy Niemack

"If you want to know what real jazz singing can be (but rarely is) listen to Judy Niemack. . . . She is a musician in the truest sense."
Dan Morgenstern
Down Beat

"Her dynamically delivered three-octave vocals soar above superb accompaniment."
Nancy Ann Lee
Jazz Times

". . . one of the best, and purest jazz singers ever . . . a voice with the clarity of a mountain stream, accuracy of pitch and time that is a wonder to hear, perfect diction and sensitivity to lyrics . . . a disciplined improvisational gift that makes her scat-sung lines music."
Safford Chamberlain
L.A. Jazz Scene

Singer Judy Niemack improvises as a pure musician, exploring jazz like a virtuoso horn player. Her scatting and delivery of lyrics are in the jazz tradition, while she breaks new ground with her original lyrics and songs and a modern approach to the standards.

She currently divides her time between Berlin and New York City, performing and giving masterclasses in Europe, Asia and the USA. As Germany's first professor of jazz voice, she headed the pop and jazz vocal department for 26 years at the Hanns Eisler Music Conservatory, later Jazz Institut Berlin, and concurrently ran the vocal jazz program in San Sebastian, Spain, for 13 years at Musikene School of Higher Music. She continues performing as a jazz vocalist and has released 15 albums so far.

Niemack was born in Pasadena, California, where she began to study classical voice at 17. At 18, friends who studied jazz with the great tenor saxophonist Warne Marsh introduced her to him, and she became fascinated with jazz improvisation. She continued her classical studies at the New England Conservatory in Boston and at the Cleveland Institute of Music, but realized that her true path lay in improvised music. She returned to California, where she sang in jazz clubs at night and studied improvisation with Marsh by day. She was his only vocal student, and he taught her as he taught horn players. When she moved to New York City in 1977, her first major engagement was a week at the Village Vanguard with him.

She has recorded fifteen CDs as a leader, with such jazz luminaries as Joey Baron, Kenny Barron, Ray Drummond, Billy Hart, Fred Hersch, Joe Lovano, Adam Nussbaum, Toots Thielemans, Mal Waldron, Cedar Walton and Kenny Werner. Her most recent CD, *What's Love?* features Judy singing ten of her original lyrics. Ken Dryden of New York's Hothouse Magazine writes:

"One of the most adventurous vocalists active, Judy Niemack's stylistic repertoire is extensive, and her infectious voice captures the essence of every song. Whether it is a standard, jazz classic, pop song, or an original composition, she always finds a fresh approach to even the most frequently recorded tunes. Over the past few years, Judy has written lyrics for numerous jazz instrumentals, especially for her Sunnyside CDs. Judy's newest album, *What's Love?,* features pianist Sullivan Fortner, guitarist Peter Bernstein, bassist Doug Weiss and drummer Joe Farnsworth."

Niemack has written and recorded several of her own songs, some of which are on https://jazzleadsheets.com/composers/judy-niemack.html. She has written lyrics for compositions by Richie Beirach, Clifford Brown, Bill Evans, Don Grolnick, Lee Konitz, Jim McNeely, Pat Metheny, Thelonious Monk, Kirk Nurock, Richie Powell, Dexter Gordon, Gigi Gryce, Larry Schneider, Steve Slagle, Peter Bernstein and Mike Stern, among others.

For more information, visit www.judyniemack.com.

Discography

As a leader

By Heart featuring Warne Marsh, Eddie Gomez (Seabreeze, 1978)

Blue Bop featuring Cedar Walton, Curtis Fuller, Ray Drummond, Joey Baron (Freelance, 1988)

Long as You're Living featuring Joe Lovano, Fred Hersch, Billy Hart (Freelance, 1990)

Heart's Desire with Kenny Barron (Stash, 1991)

Straight Up featuring Toots Thielemans, Kenny Werner, Adam Nussbaum, Mark Feldman, Jeanfrançois Prins (Freelance, 1993)

Mingus, Monk and Mal duet with Mal Waldron (Freelance, 1994)

. . . Night and the Music featuring Kenny Werner, Jeanfrançois Prins, Ray Drummond, Billy Hart, Eric Friedlander (Freelance, 1996)

About Time featuring Eddie Gomez, Jeanfrançois Prins, Lee Konitz, David Friedman, Edson da Silva (Café) (Sony Jazz, 2003)

Jazz Singer's Practice Session featuring Fred Hersch, Scott Colley, Dick Weller (GAM, 2003)

Blue Nights featuring Don Sickler, Gary Bartz, Jim McNeely, Jeanfrancois Prins, Dennis Irwin, Victor Lewis (Blujazz, 2007)

In the Sundance featuring Bruce Barth, Jeanfrancois Prins, Rufus Reid, Bruno Castellucci (Blujazz, 2009)

Listening To You featuring Dan Tepfer (Sunnyside 2012)

New York Stories featuring Jim McNeely & The Danish Radio Big Band (Sunnyside, 2018)

Sing Your Song duo with Wolfgang Koehler (Contemplate 2019)

What's Love? featuring Peter Bernstein, Sullivan Fortner (Sunnyside 2022)

As a guest (selected discography)

Beauty and the Prince with Jeanfrançois Prins featuring Fred Hersch, Hein van de Geyn, Bruno Castellucci (AMC, 1993)

Rhapsody Volumes 1 and 2 with Lee Konitz (Paddle Wheel, 1993)

The Other Side of Walter Boeykens (distributed by Sony, 1994)

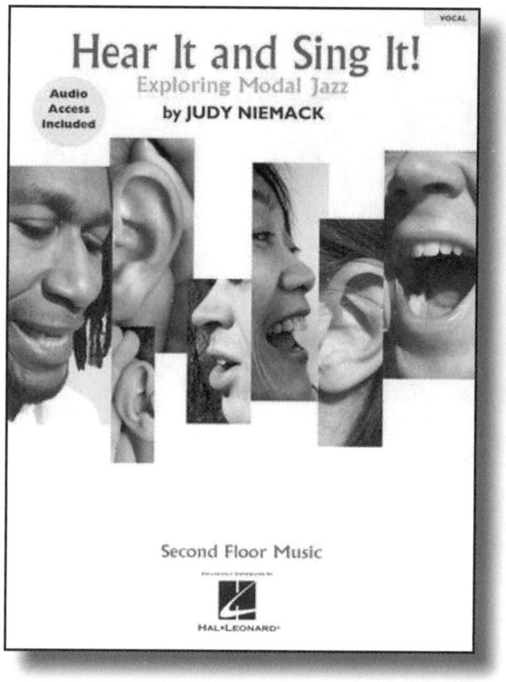

Explore Modal Jazz with Judy Niemack's
Hear It and Sing It!
Exploring Modal Jazz
It's a fun and effective way to improve your vocal technique and internalize the basic scales used in jazz.

Learn to sing the blues with Judy Niemack's
Hear It and Sing It!
Exploring the Blues
A great tool for learning to sing and improvise on the blues while exploring songs by jazz masters with lyrics by Judy Niemack.

Get Judy's books from your local music dealer or online at Hal Leonard.com.

Sing JAZZ! presents 76 titles by jazz lyricists and instrumentalists, including many classic jazz compositions by legendary artists, now with lyrics

An in-depth exploration of jazz phrasing including many different ways to approach ***I'm Movin' On*** (Kurt Nurock, Judy Niemack). Examples sung by Judy Niemack.

Whether you're a karaoke singer or preparing for an audition, the Hal Leonard Pro Vocal series is for you. Eight classic songs with demos by Judy along with backing tracks.